# ENDOR

This is a must-read for anyone interested in living a life filled with successful, fruitful, win-win relationships both personal and professional. While there is growing focus and training on managing relationships via the 2 dimensional tools of social media, it's refreshing to see some guidance in the 3rd dimension, namely face-to-face interaction. This is a true road map to success and should be required reading for all B-school students and politicians.

—Jeff Gubala
V.P. Mutual Funds and Managed Accounts
Westwood Holdings Co.

From the first quote to the final exercises in the Appendix, *The 9 Dimensions of Conscious Success* succeeds in establishing relevance for your life's journey. David Nielson uses a combination of survey results, common sense, examples, and exercises to structure a practical process to grow a career...and a life. I highly recommend this book to individuals and to groups to use as an effective tool for self awareness and collaborative conversations.

—Faye W. Gilbert, Ph.D.
Dean, College of Business
The University of Southern Mississippi

In *The 9 Dimensions of Conscious Success*, David Nielson's study brings practical clarity to what it takes to be successful and how to consciously work toward your success. The lessons in this book will serve any reader well, as have all of my engagements with David Nielson.

—Kathryn King, PhD
Vice President, Clinical Research
Levo Therapeutics, Inc

*The 9 Dimensions of Conscious Success—It's All About YOU!* is an excellent book and just what is needed to help Millennials chart their course to success. I've had the pleasure of working with David for over 20 years—his keen insights into organizations and how to perform at the highest level, make this book a must read for anyone. The book and the Conscious Success Assessment are great tools for anyone in business today.

—MICHAEL J MENARD
President, The Gensight Group Inc.

I have completed reading Mr. Nielson's book, *The 9 Dimensions of Conscious Success*. It is rare that I can find a book to keep my attention, but I hardly could stop reading Mr. Nielson's book. The training that we received yesterday was second-to-none. At this point in my life where I am trying to figure out which path I would like to take, the training from Mr. Nielson and Mr. Bracey has provided me with an even bigger desire to overcome life's obstacles and conquer success.

—JOSH SPIVEY
Senior, The University of Southern Mississippi

*The 9 Dimensions of Conscious Success* encourages you and shows you how to grow personally and professionally, define your purpose, and gain self and social awareness. This book gives you confidence that you can make conscious decisions on how to be the best you. The impact is extraordinary.

—VICTORIA BEYEA
The University of Southern Mississippi

$3 + 6$

THE **9 DIMENSIONS** OF
# CONSCIOUS
# SUCCESS

*It's All About YOU!*

# DAVID E. NIELSON

*David E. Nielson* (signature)

SOUND WISDOM

P.O. Box 310

Shippensburg, PA 17257-0310

For more information on publishing and distribution rights, call 717-530-2122 or info@soundwisdom.com

**Quantity Sales.** Special discounts are available on quantity purchases by corporations, associations, and others. For details, contact the Sales Department at Sound Wisdom.

While efforts have been made to verify information contained in this publication, neither the author nor the publisher assumes any responsibility for errors, inaccuracies, or omissions.

While this publication is chock-full of useful, practical information; it is not intended to be legal or accounting advice. All readers are advised to seek competent lawyers and accountants to follow laws and regulations that may apply to specific situations.

The reader of this publication assumes responsibility for the use of the information. The author and publisher assume no responsibility or liability whatsoever on the behalf of the reader of this publication.

ISBN 13 TP: 978-1-64095-003-0

ISBN 13 eBook: 978-1-64095-004-7

For Worldwide Distribution, Printed in the U.S.A.

Cover/Jacket designer Eileen Rockwell

Interior design by Terry Clifton

1 2 3 4 5 6 7 8 / 22 21 20 19 18

*Library of Congress Cataloging-in-Publication Data*

Names: Nielson, David E., author.

Title: The nine dimensions of conscious success : it's all about YOU! / David E. Nielson.

Other titles: 9 dimensions of conscious success

Description: Shippensburg : Sound Wisdom, 2018.

Identifiers: LCCN 2017041937| ISBN 9781640950030 (paperback) | ISBN 9781640950047 (ebook)

Subjects: LCSH: Success. | Success in business. | Self-actualization (Psychology) | BISAC: SELF-HELP / Personal Growth / General. | BUSINESS & ECONOMICS / Motivational.

Classification: LCC BF637.S8 N484 2018 | DDC 650.1--dc23

LC record available at https://lccn.loc.gov/2017041937

*This book is dedicated to three people:*

*My father, for teaching me and then modeling how to best show up in life!*

*My mother, for giving me the best compass for life!*

*My wife, June Elizabeth, for inspiring me to be a better person every day!*

# ACKNOWLEDGMENTS

I TRULY STAND ON THE SHOULDERS OF GIANTS. I'M GRATEFUL
to so many for their influence and help with this book.

I heard my dad's voice a lot as I wrote—I think of him
every day and I feel like he's still with me.

Thanks to older sisters Sue and Linda who worked hard
growing up to ensure I never lost my understanding of the
seniority system.

I thank John Jones (long past) and Hyler Bracey as two of
the most significant influences in my life. In very caring ways
they both taught me so much and modeled everything they
taught—in itself a key lesson. Their voices are prominent in
the content.

I especially appreciate all the individuals who contributed
by being will to be interviewed by me. Their insights and
responses form a very solid foundation for what I'm proposing.

I thank my new friends at Sound Wisdom, the publisher
who provide what the name implies. They provided cogent
insights about the content and great advice and help with the
manuscript. Could not have brought this to market without the
help of David Wildasin and John Martin.

My thanks to Scott Snyder for his experience and insights into the world of publishing and for being a sounding board.

My thanks to our Personal Assistant, Maureen Sullivan for all she does to keep our life in order. That was a huge help while doing this.

Finally, my thanks go to my many clients—especially those who became friends—for helping me on my personal learning journey for the past 24 years. All those valuable discussions served as guideposts on the path to this final product.

# CONTENTS

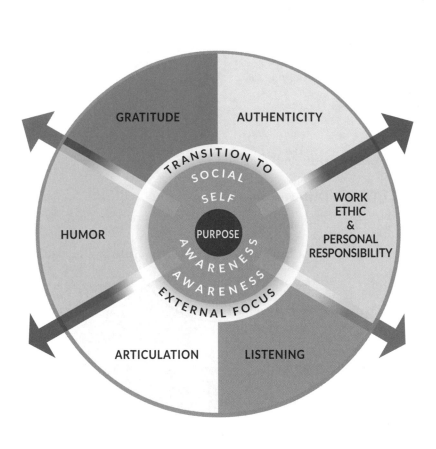

# FOREWORD

## by Ken Blanchard

WHEN DAVID NIELSON ASKED ME TO WRITE THE FOREWORD to *The 9 Dimensions of Conscious Success*, I was pleased for several reasons. For one thing, success is important to everyone I know. There are a lot of books about achieving it, but to my knowledge none follow logical steps—particularly steps that begin with a sense of purpose and self-awareness.

Why is it important to begin with these two elements? Because until you know your real purpose in life *and* understand who you are as a unique individual, the success you pursue could end up being the flavor of the month. David follows with the third foundational element—social awareness. This is where you watch the environment around you so that you are aware of how people are affected by what you say and do. Remember, relationships are just as important—if not more important—than results.

Once you have the *elements* that form the foundation for success—a sense of purpose, a sense of self, and an awareness of how you affect people in the social systems around you—David introduces six *differentiators* that will help you transition from where you are to where you want to be. Three of these jump out at me.

- *Listening.* I've always liked the saying "If God wanted us to speak more than listen he would have given us two mouths." Listening is a skill most of us need to work on.

- I also love that David includes *Humor* as one of his six differentiators. To me, the most successful people take what they do seriously but themselves lightly. Humorless people are just not fun or interesting to be around.

- The other differentiator that really resonates with me is *Gratitude.* Research shows that when you are in a stressful situation, if you stop and think about what you are thankful for, the stress will subside. Stress and gratitude cannot exist together.

As you read this book, you'll also learn about the other three differentiators: *Authenticity, Work Ethic and Personal Responsibility,* and *Articulation.* David goes deep to describe all 9 dimensions, giving examples of how and why they are necessary in the big picture.

Thanks, David, for showing us that we are our best selves when we realize there is a better way than trial and error to plot our course in life and achieve our ultimate level of success.

KEN BLANCHARD
Coauthor of *The New One Minute Manager*®
and coeditor of *Servant Leadership in Action*

My thanks to Ken for this Foreword. Perhaps best known for *Situational Leadership* and *The One-Minute Manager*, Ken has written or co-written over 60 books and is a giant in the field of training and development.

# INTRODUCTION

ACHIEVING SUCCESS IS A VERY PERSONAL CHALLENGE IN THE twenty-first century. Trial and error is neither the best nor an efficient option anymore. The most efficient way to find your way to the top is with a structured approach that accelerates the process by stressing a conscious self-awareness of what you really want in life.

> "The greatest glory in living lies not in never falling, but in rising every time we fall."
> —NELSON MANDELA, *Long Walk to Freedom*

Great quote—that leads me to a great yet painfully personal example.

When I was in my late twenties, I joined a group going to Lake Powell for a week of house-boating and waterskiing. As I recall, beer drinking was also a major part of the plan. I was excited because these would all be new experiences for me (except the beer drinking!). I'd never been to Lake Powell, a place I really wanted to see. Furthermore, I was very excited to learn how to waterski. I thought most of the ingredients were in place for a good time. Back then, I was fairly athletic, coordinated, and very active; and accomplished skiers were going to teach me. We had great boats and lots of good equipment. It seemed like a recipe for success.

I awoke on the second day thrilled about my first waterskiing experience. The ski boats were ready and we were out on a glassy, smooth lake. I was eager for instruction but wasn't given much. Mostly as an afterthought, two of the experienced skiers said, "This is really a breeze—you'll pick it up naturally!" After suiting me up in a lifejacket, slipping my feet into two skis, and getting into the water behind the boat, I was given the following very informal tips:

1.  Point the ski tips up; hold the towrope *very tightly* with two hands. You really have to hang on or the rope will be ripped out of your hands when the boat takes off.

2.  Bend your knees between your arms, ski tips up.

3.  When the boat takes off, hold on tightly.

4.  When the boat reaches speed, just stand up with your feet and skis about two feet apart.

5   Hold on tightly to the rope.

Seemed simple enough. I thought I'd be skiing on the first try. It turns out that it was slightly more complex than what I expected. There is a certain balance and feel that is quite important. It took me about five tries to actually stand and ski. After that it was fairly natural and fun. However, in addition to the instructions about what I *should do,* it turns out it might have been helpful to tell me a few things I should *not* do! For example, beginners should never try to waterski on their faces—it's painful.

The first two tries I fell, but I didn't let go of the towrope, which caused the boat to drag me for a while—my body flopping around a bit like a rag doll being dragged behind a car. It was very entertaining for my friends in the boat—less so for me. That first time they stopped "fairly" quickly and circled back around to me.

They gave me more tips: "Straighten your arms," "Stand up more slowly," "Lean back," etc. I was ready for my second try. I was all set up, and the boat took off. Same result—a fall, more face skiing, and more flopping around. The boat came back around, and I received more coaching; but this time, one of my "friends" between fits of laughter said, "Hey Dave, here's a new idea—if you fall, let go of the rope!" More bouts of laughter from my other so-called friends who were all accomplished skiers. It makes me smile now to think back on it. Being a source of entertainment for others sometimes has a certain appeal— years down the road.

That thing about letting go of the rope seems obvious now, but I had no frame of reference for waterskiing at the time. I could eventually see the humor in it all—especially after I could stand and actually enjoy the water sport.

Concentrating on holding tightly to the rope apparently superseded any other logic in the case of falling. Additionally, when "in the moment," especially in foreign or uncomfortable territory, it's hard to be aware and logical. I really wasn't very aware of anything other than that rope being an important link to the boat.

# In Retrospect

In retrospect, two key aspects to learning this sport were missing. First, there was not enough real structure for success. The instructions were too sparse and informal, which forced a lot of trial and error. There was no real framework such as, "Do these five things and avoid these five things." I believe my friends had good intentions; they just neglected to be more specific. I had been a golf instructor earlier in my life, so I knew the value of creating an instruction structure that would produce a repeated, practiced pattern. That was missing.

Second, consciousness was missing. I was trying to rely on my natural athletic ability and watching others. I was not conscious in my approach, and without consciousness it is hard to make corrections (especially as you are being dragged around a lake!).

This book is about a number of important concepts; at a meta level, it is about awareness and consciousness. Mostly, it is about the right combination of structure and conscious behaviors required for success, especially in all endeavors with others. You will read about practical actions you can take to be more effective when interrelating with others to achieve success.

Remember, as was true in my waterskiing lesson, success seems a slow, difficult road at first, but this perspective changes quickly as you continue learning. Consider the words of economist Rudi Dornbusch who noted, "Things take longer to happen than you think they will, and then they happen faster than you thought they could."

# What? So What? Now What?

One of my friends and mentors in life was a great man by the name of John Joncs who co-founded University Associates—a successful publishing and training company. He taught me many things, but one of his nuggets was how to organize thoughts, presentations, meeting agendas, etc. He used the structure "What? So What? Now What?" to explain easy as well as hard-to-grasp ideas. So in this book, I will be sharing with you:

- **What?** Nine vital dimensions of conscious success.

- **So What?** These dimensions are important if you want to experience a greater level of achievement and accomplishment in your business, career, and personal relationships.

- **Now What?** Now you apply what you've learned by using the self-scored assessment and then the practical applications provided at the end of each chapter. These strategies, activities, and further points to ponder assist you in making positive life changes *today*.

Considering all of the "success" books available today, none address the particular combination of skills and behaviors for success that are in this book. I've put together what I think is the definitive list. This is a set of proven, closely interrelated, synergistic actions that will make you more effective and thereby more successful in business and in life.

Perhaps as important is providing you with a tool to measure those skills and behaviors. We will provide more information on the self-scored assessment soon.

# Three Parts

There are three parts to the book. *First,* the *Conscious Success Model* is offered for an initial examination with in-depth discussions throughout the following chapters. Also, I lay out a *case for change* by exposing the current environment and relevant research on barriers to success. In comparing my journey to those entering the world of work today, it is obvious that conditions are more difficult now—yet universal realities apply then and now and in the future, which I bring to your attention.

In the *second* part, I share with you *Nine Success Dimensions* that are the results of research I conducted and distilled down to key patterns that validate the effective direction, skills, and behaviors I advocate. I provide a *success foundation of three internal characteristics*; add to that *six crucial differentiators* that distinguish you from everyone else—critical to success and personal effectiveness.

In the *final* part, I outline how you can *move forward on a conscious, deliberate improvement journey.* The Appendices contain survey results from interviewing successful people and a true-life inspirational story you won't soon forget.

SECTION 1

# THE CASE FOR CHANGE

# CHAPTER 1

# MANAGING LIFE

*"Life is difficult."*

DR. M. SCOTT PECK BEGAN HIS BESTSELLING BOOK *The Road Less Traveled* with these words: "Life is difficult." I started reading the book during a difficult time in my life. Its impactful message of journeying toward a higher level of self-understanding became clear to me then and is even clearer to me now.

This whole notion of life being difficult started me thinking. When I was growing up, we were taught to work hard and that there would be fruits to our labors. We could have a good, steady job with a company, buy an affordable home, and achieve the lifestyle we would like.

Life was hard, but it was not overwhelmingly difficult. Life was a game that had definite rules—the amount of effort equaled the amount of return. If you worked hard, you would have enough money to support and raise a family, hopefully own your own home, and even pay it off by retirement time.

To some, this might sound like some utopian-themed black-and-white TV sitcom. Things have changed. Life has become more difficult and complicated because of the fluidity of life now. People change jobs much more frequently; technology and communication is evolving at a very fast pace, and young people have to be willing to not only keep up with all the changes but move forward deliberately, consciously.

When I consider those who are just now starting out—either readying for college or another path or beginning a career—I get a bit nostalgic and concerned. It seems life's degree of difficulty is significantly higher now than previous times, but if equipped to make wise and conscious decisions there is every probability your journey will be exciting as well as productive and fruitful.

## Life's Degree of Difficulty

*Warning: The information you are about to read may be alarming!*

For example, inflation puts us all at the mercy of the almighty dollar. Simply put, the cost of food, energy, and shelter has increased over time. According to the Bureau of Labor Statistics, Consumer Price Index, an item that cost $100 in 1980 now would cost more than $291.55. That is a 191 percent increase.[1]

## Then and Now Costs[2]

### 1980

- Average monthly rent: $300
- Average cost of new home: $68,700
- Gas: $1.19
- Car: $7,900
- Loaf of bread: 50 cents

### 2016

- Average monthly rent: $1,213.13 (300% increase)
- Average cost of new home: $188,900 (175% increase)
- Gas: $2.31 (94% increase)
- Car: $ 22,000 (178% increase)
- Loaf of bread: $2.32 (364% increase)

## Statistics from the United States Census Bureau:

### 1980

- Median household income, adjusted for inflation: $48,462

### 2014

- Median household income, adjusted for inflation: $53,013

That is a $5,000 difference, but the cost of living has sky-rocketed. Here are a couple of other numbers to consider:

- Number of households in 1980: 82,368,000
- Number of households in 2014: 124,587,000

In 2008, the unemployment rate reached the highest level in more than fourteen years. In eighteen months, 3.3 million workers were added to the jobless rolls. The economy was in a deep recession with millions of working families unable to find jobs.[3]

When the economy rebounded, new jobs were created and new businesses emerged, which prompted viable competition between people searching for desirable positions. Now that more people are employed, there are more people competing for the jobs they want. Just like you.

What becomes important now is how you can *differentiate* yourself among those competing for their own success. That is one of the key principles discussed in this book—being bold and standing out in your chosen endeavor in order to get the respect, recognition, and opportunities you want and deserve. In short, to achieve the success you want.

## Competitive Edge

How do you compete in today's market? How do you stand out among the vast sea of eligible candidates? One of the main ways is through education. Having an Ivy League pedigree sounds great, if you have the wallet for it. But is it really the differentiator it once was?

I'm a big believer in the idea that most people should give college a try. It was a tremendous experience for me (I remember most of it!), and it can help develop an individual in many ways beyond academics.

Start first by determining what your passion might be. One big challenge now is that college educations are outrageously expensive and beyond the reach of many.

I'm not suggesting that an education is not important. It could be very important depending on your goals. What I am suggesting is that it takes more than college credentials to ensure your success.

Regardless of the university attended and the exemplary grades earned, that means very little if people lack the basic skills and behaviors that enhance their ability to interact effectively with other human beings. No matter how smart they are, the failure to form effective interpersonal relationships to achieve a common goal is always a handicap. Regardless of outstanding qualifications on paper, they will not be as great as they could be if they lack the skills and characteristics to work well with others.

## From Grim to Exciting

So far I have painted a pretty grim picture while providing some context for the life-is-difficult fact. Today we are expected to know more, produce more, and produce it faster. But obviously, many are making it, so what do they do differently? How do they get noticed?

There is an old adage, "What got you where you are won't take you where you want to go." I agree. There must be a new strategy based on proven past experiences—and that is what you will learn in this and the following chapters.

When I look at my successful career and the world of work in general, it is clear that every job involves interaction with others at various levels. In most workplaces, there are frequent interactions between coworkers, management, clients, etc. Teams are a common element in most companies.

## Show Me the Way

This book explores being present, being noticed, and most importantly, how to be consciously successful. So how you *show up* in life is a conscious choice—an important choice, it turns out.

My father was a significant influence and friend throughout my life. When I was young, he was great at "showing me the way"—even showing me "a better way" if he thought the path I was on was leading me toward trouble. He wasn't overprotective; he was helpful. Like a lot of young kids, I wasn't always paying attention to my parents when they provided direction.

When Dad wanted to ensure I heard and understood his advice, he packaged it within a "memorable mnemonic" such as, "David, use your head for something other than a hat rack." That would be followed by a tip or some good advice and encouraging me to *"Think* before you act!" I always smiled when he said that. Thinking before we act increases self-awareness and leads to higher consciousness of the moment.

"Think before you act!"

I'm careful not to represent these ideas as new—although many may seem new to you. We have enormous capacity for learning, but most importantly we have truly enormous capacity for *relearning!* Some of the most profound aspects of life you already know—you learned them at a young age, but perhaps you haven't considered their value in your current circumstances.

In this book, I present a set of necessary skills and behaviors for the world in which you live and work. In short, I offer a *framework for conscious success!* This framework is universally useful yet lacking in many people in today's world. This model is offered to everyone of any age who wants to advance in their career, business—life. If you have a pulse, you qualify and can benefit from continuing to read.

## Lessons Learned

I recently had lunch with my two older sisters, and we talked about how great it was to have grown up when we did—when life was far simpler.

When I consider my life's journey to the present, my first reaction is how fortunate I've been. I have tremendous gratitude for the lessons I learned and am sharing with you now. I had a great childhood; a solid, fun college experience; and then went to work full time. I had a successful career in the corporate world and since then have achieved success as an independent management consultant.

> I am absolutely convinced that my success is due more to skills picked up along the way based on self-awareness.

I'm naturally curious, and so it's normal for me to wonder what contributed to any success I've had and how it is different from the experiences of others. I am absolutely convinced that any success I've had is far less due to my college degree and more due to skills I've picked up along the way based on increasing my self-awareness. A lot more discussion on that in a bit.

I've met many people over the years who are smarter, in some cases *much* smarter, than I am, but they have not achieved the level of success I've experienced. What made the difference? When I examine those situations, I can point to one or more of the elements discussed in this book as the cause of not achieving their full potential.

> Luck is not a strategic plan, and trial and error is not an effective process.

I didn't think much about *consciousness* for many years of my life. I wasn't very aware or deliberate (remember my waterskiing experience!). I had almost no sense of purpose, I had low self-awareness, and I was also socially unaware. I was just sort of stumbling through life. I suppose I was "lucky" in some aspects, but relying on luck is not the most strategic approach. It is a high-risk approach with an increased incidence of failure.

## Conscious Competence Model

According to Noel Burch, a *conscious competence model* is a continuum that illustrates how most people learn something new:

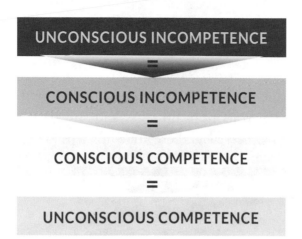

Learning to drive a car for the very first time is a good example:

1.  We start in *unconscious incompetence*—we don't know what we don't know.

2.  Through trial or education, we learn about what we don't know; now we may be *consciously incompetent*—we know what we don't know.

3.  Through practice, usually with some instruction and knowledge, we can arrive at *conscious competence*.

4.  Through "overlearning" and habit, we get to *unconscious competence*.

All of this involves self-awareness—more about that in a bit.

In moments of clarity when I look back to what was successful for me, some definite patterns emerge. To that, there is a wonderful adage, which I cite often:

"Good judgment comes from experience and a
lot of experience comes from bad judgment."

In my younger days, I must have had a lot of experience because I sure demonstrated a lot of bad judgment! I've learned a lot over the years from mistakes and bad decisions; now I strive to help others avoid those same missteps.

> Walk through life with purpose
> along a well-thought-out path.

If you are open to learning from your mistakes, that's great. You can gain a lot by being aware. But you can learn a lot more and less painfully by being proactive. First, take off the blindfold and be conscious of yourself and your environment. Then, walk through life with purpose along a well-thought-out path.

I know the learning curve can be shortened with the proper structure and direction—that's been proven repeatedly by successful people for decades. In my own case, I could have saved myself (and others around me) a lot of headaches. I will provide a pathway, or roadmap, to the critical components of being successful in the current landscape.

## What Kind of Animal Is Success?

Let's start with the concept of success. The *Oxford English Dictionary* definition is "the accomplishment of an aim or purpose."[4]

What is key about this definition is that it is quite broad, allowing you to define success in terms that are meaningful to you. It may or may not have anything to do with position, title, wealth, lifestyle, acquisitions, etc. Another key element of the definition of success is the word *purpose*. I talk a lot about purpose, and in particular *living your life on purpose*. There are at least two meanings to that phrase:

1. Living your life with intent, not accidentally or capriciously.

2. Living your life according to a carefully defined purpose you have consciously considered, planned, and documented. Literally, it is having a purpose statement. In Appendix B, you will find a copy of my own purpose.

My personal focus is examining success and being able to produce it proactively for myself. That might be a challenging enough assignment by itself—even more so when the barriers to achieve it are significant.

So think about what your own definition of success is! Make a conscious effort to define it in practical and concrete terms.

> "Whether you believe you can do a thing or not, you are right."
>
> —HENRY FORD

## Attitude

Before we jump off into the *what* and *how* of conscious success, I want to give a nod to an important overarching notion—*positive attitude*. I was blessed to have mentors and influences in my life who were pretty universally positive. I've seen firsthand that a positive outlook generally frames everything in a better light. Even under dire circumstances, a positive attitude helps minimize the negative and acts as a catalyst to move toward something better.

Certainly much has been written on this subject, and perhaps it's a very old idea, but that doesn't negate the importance of it. Attitude is a personal choice. I choose to respond, "Terrific!" when someone asks how I am. I authentically see things in my life as being terrific and say affirmations each week to reinforce that positive outlook. For some that is easier said than done—I get that. But it *is* a choice, so I encourage you to choose a positive attitude. We can't leave it there, however, because: 1. it makes for a very short book; and 2. I believe there are several tactics that will dramatically improve your probability of success against some tall odds of negativity.

So now on to my research into conscious success.

## A Look Outside My Box

My curiosity about this notion of success, particularly conscious success, had me thinking. I observed what the elements of my own success were and how my self-awareness was a key element. But was I unique? Or was I just making correlations between ideas and connecting them in ways that fit my thesis?

If I wished to teach others what constitutes conscious success and develop a model that worked to support and develop that awareness, I had to reach outside my box and ask others.

A man I admired greatly once told me a story about a talk he had given to his newly formed team shortly after he had been promoted. He was encouraging teamwork and the notion of the strength of the group.

He said, "Look folks, about the only thing I can really do by myself is go to the bathroom."

Perhaps that's a bit "earthy," but it was a memorable way to make the point. Famous author, mentor, and servant leader Ken Blanchard likes to say that "None of us is as smart as all of us."

## Validating and Generating

Central to the success of a lot of individual ideas is validating the idea with others. A very helpful process is to seek advice from those we trust when faced with important decisions. I've been very fortunate in life to have met and spent time with really great people. So I decided to tap into that great resource to validate my own ideas and generate some new ones.

I thought about people I knew who were successful, and I developed questions as a basis for interviews I would conduct. I was looking for patterns that not only supported my notion but also developed a premise around which I could create a model. Then I would share those conclusions with readers like you who could learn from my research and not have to reinvent the success wheel.

I'm very grateful to all the people who took the time with me to be interviewed. Their valuable contributions are woven throughout this book.

I began this chapter with the phrase, "Life is difficult." Although life can be difficult at times, my intent is to make life less difficult by giving you an advantage. You can compete and succeed easier and faster using new tools, new ideas, and new strategies.

In each chapter, you will be presented with concepts that may take you some time to digest. To assist in that absorption of ideas, there is a practical application section: "Now what?" This section includes strategies, activities, and further points to ponder. The following is your first *Now what?* to consider. You may want to have a notebook handy to record your answers, feelings, and actions you want to take in response.

## Now What?

1.  What are your goals for success? How are you defining them? Are you considering things other than career and money in those goals?

2.  What are your current challenges? Not enough time? Not enough money? No ability to advance? Write these down. As you progress through this book, you will begin to find strategies for solving these issues.

3.  If you attended college, is having the degree producing the results you want, the success for which you strive?

4.  Is your college experience differentiating you enough to achieve your success goals?

5   What other ways can you leverage your talents to make money without the need for further education? What are you passionate about? Are you passionate about the work you do? If not, how could you build a business around your passion?

"I am here for a purpose and that purpose is to grow into a *mountain,* not to shrink to a grain of sand. Henceforth will I apply *all* my efforts to become the highest mountain of all and I will strain my potential until it cries for mercy."

—Og Mandino,
*The Greatest Salesman in the World*

# CHAPTER 2

# THE STUDY

*"Individual commitment to a group effort—*
*that is what makes a team work, a company*
*work, a society work, a civilization work."*
—VINCE LOMBARDI

CONSISTENT WITH THE IDEA THAT INDIVIDUALS COMMITTED
to a common goal can produce great results, I knew I wanted
to hear ideas outside of my frame of reference in writing this
book. I thought about great people I had encountered in my life
and started a list of people who would give me great insights. I
set out to contact and interview them after developing a list of
five questions.

I don't want to give the impression that this was a formal,
scientifically structured study. I did not have a control group or
blind responses.

I just wanted to know from people whom I deemed "successful" what they thought were the elements of a successful leader.

The following are the questions I asked. Please take some time and answer them for yourself. In the back of the book (Appendix D), you will find an answer sheet provided which can serve as an important worksheet for you as you go through this book:

- **Question 1**: Think of one or two very successful (in business and life) individuals you've witnessed/admired in your career. What two or three personality traits in those successful individuals do you believe most contributed to their success?

- **Question 2**: What two or three qualities or personality traits have most contributed to your own success in business and in life?

- **Question 3**: What behaviors or personality traits do you believe most hinder others in being successful in life and in business?

- **Question 4**: When considering one of your most challenging times or a time when you made a mistake and had to deal with it in the best way, what action or characteristic or thought helped you get through the adversity?

- **Question 5**: What are the one or two most important pieces of advice you would give to the next generation to improve their impact on our world in the future?

# Interview Data Themes

In Appendix A, I provide some of the top responses I received. No one was privileged to see another person's answers, so when I saw a lot of duplication between the different interviewee's answers, I paid attention. Many of the answers were the same when defining success and what skills made them successful. The values were evident.

One word in Question 3 was prevalent. The word? *Lack.* There were essential qualities lacking in people who were not successful. There are "toolbelt qualities" that successful people must have as part of their authentic makeup—honesty, integrity, trustworthiness, for examples. These qualities are stronger than the assumption that a person is doing something wrong or has developed a bad habit. Rather, they lack some key ingredient—their *sine qua non* ("without which, there is nothing")—"something absolutely indispensable or essential; reliability is a *sine qua non* for success."[1]

The question that came to mind—how do people gain those traits? It's not as if they can go to the corner store and buy them. Are we born with the traits, or can the traits be developed?

# Piecing the Puzzle Together

When solving a jigsaw puzzle, people have different techniques for figuring out how it all goes together. No matter the method, each piece has to be considered to fill a hole in the overall image. To find the right fit, different angles have to be considered. Once each piece is placed in its correct position, a clear picture emerges. By the way, it is much easier to complete a jigsaw puzzle if you refer to the image on the box top so you know what the end result is supposed to look like. This is akin to defining your purpose.

Going through the responses from these questions was much the same as piecing together a puzzle. There were many similar answers, but where did the pieces go to create a cohesive model of success?

Where were the patterns? Where did the pieces belong? Were there patterns on the pieces that gave clues to a clear end result?

I looked at each of the answers and turned them around in my head. I discovered that today's successful people are worried about the upcoming generation's ability to be successful and to be strong leaders. They see the younger generation through seasoned lenses and realize that today's values and beliefs are different from past generations. Yet the basics remain the same for yesterday, today, and tomorrow.

No one sets out to fail.

No one sets out to fail in life. No one goes into the world with the aim to become nothing. It is true that some may give up along the way, but most people desire a sense of achievement and self-worth. Success is a wonderful experience—no matter if succeeding at waterskiing or sealing a multimillion-dollar deal—so most seek success with a passion.

The difference between us is our journey to get there. Some say, "Be true to yourself, follow your passion, and make your way." Albert Einstein said, "Try not to become a man of success, but try rather to become a man of value." And Leonardo da Vinci has been credited as saying, "It had long since come to my attention that people of accomplishment rarely sat back and let things happen to them. They went out and happened to things."

The models that grew out of these questions and answers were created to develop tools and a matrix of success to help you move forward toward accomplishing your goals that will lead you to success. Each tool and matrix presented work for any and every generation when absorbed into your personal style and being.

We curmudgeons are a bit self-serving in our advice. We know the time is coming soon when we will rely on you to take care of the world—and us for as long as we are in it. We want you to succeed because you are our legacy. Whether we are your parent, your teacher, your coach, your mentor, or your Pilates teacher, we want, no, we *need* you to succeed because your success is our success. Our greatest fault, though, is the notion that our way is the only way. Our way is *one* way you can choose, but by no means is it the only way.

> We want you to succeed because you are our legacy.

By adopting the model presented in the next chapter that is based on the compiled interview data, you can live life in a fully aware and conscious way. It will help you develop the core values that will expedite your journey toward success while at the same time allow you to explore, be creative, and recover quickly from failure—because it is the lessons learned from failure that really allow you to grow.

> "Far better is it to dare mighty things, to win glorious triumphs, even though checkered by failure...than to rank with those poor spirits who neither enjoy nor suffer much, because they live in a gray twilight that knows not victory nor defeat."
> —TEDDY ROOSEVELT, "The Strenuous Life"

## Patterns Discovered

After I had all of the answers, distinct patterns began to emerge. Some were easy to see because the same words were repeated over and over between people and between different questions.

I categorized the answers into twelve categories:

1. Purpose

2. Belief Systems and Values

3. Social Awareness

4. Application and Implementation

5 Communication and Listening

6. Leadership and Mentorship

7. Flexibility

8. Humility

9. Knowledge

10. Self-Awareness

11. Support System

12. Independence

In Appendix A is a complete list of how the answers fell into each of those categories for each question, with the top three categories for each question listed below.

Some of the people's answers had parts that landed into more than one category. Some of the questions did not have every category represented. Let's look at the top three categories for each question.

**Question 1:** Think of one or two very successful (in business and life) individuals you've witnessed/admired in your career. What two or three personality traits in those successful individuals do you believe most contributed to their success?

- Purpose: 33

- Social Awareness: 27

- Belief Systems and Values: 25

**Question 2:** What two or three qualities or personality traits have most contributed to your own success in business and in life?

- Purpose: 46

- Application and Implementation: 19

- Social Awareness: 21

**Question 3:** What behaviors or personality traits do you believe most hinder others in being successful in life and in business?

- Belief Systems and Values: 25

- Social Awareness: 23

- Purpose: 20

**Question 4:** When considering one of your most challenging times or a time when you made a mistake and had to deal with it in the best way, what action or characteristic or thought helped you get through the adversity?

- Belief Systems and Values: 35

- Purpose: 25

- Support System: 14

**Question 5:** What are the one or two most important pieces of advice you would give to the next generation to improve their impact on our world in the future?

- Purpose: 20

- Social Awareness: 20

- Belief Systems and Values: 19

I added all the numbers together for each of the categories to finally see what the most important aspects of being successful really are, according to the people interviewed. I knew this final calculation would help me determine what would made the cut and what would not.

- Purpose: 144

- Belief Systems and Values: 122

- Social Awareness: 94

- Application and Implementation: 67

- Communication and Listening: 62

- Leadership and Mentorship: 55

- Flexibility: 54

- Humility: 53

- Knowledge: 46

- Self-Awareness: 33

- Support System: 14

- Independence: 2

Can you guess from the list which ones I kept and which ones I tossed? Take a minute and consider each one. Flip to the next page when you are ready for the answer.

**If you guessed that I kept all of them, you are correct.** Like the puzzle I've been referring to, *every piece,* no matter how small or plain, *is important.* They all come together to make the complete picture. Every aspect of success on that list is important. Remember, I told you that each person has to navigate his or her own path and find the way that works best. Each person needs something different at different times.

While I did not cut any, I sorted them and came up with two different models, each one supporting the other. Then it was time to integrate what I learned from others and what I knew from my own life and professional experiences. I'm excited to share with you the results and know you will benefit from the work.

# Now What?

1.  Now review your answers to the five questions mentioned in this chapter. How do your answers compare to the interviewees' answers? This begins your self-awareness process in understanding how you see success.

2.  Into which categories do you think your answers fit? How do yours compare?

    ■ Purpose

    ■ Belief Systems and Values

    ■ Social Awareness

    ■ Application and Implementation

    ■ Communication and Listening

- Leadership and Mentorship

- Flexibility

- Humility

- Knowledge

- Self-Awareness

- Support System

- Independence

3. Ask other people the questions and consider their answers. This is a great way to get to know your boss, coworkers, and even your clients.

4. To make any survey more credible, a large pool of people is best. Please consider sending me your answers so I can add them to my ever-growing survey sample. Your answers are kept confidential, just as the ones appearing in this book. To complete your free assessment, visit www.conscioussuccess.com.

5 How did you compare? Look at the themes from my interviews in the Appendix and compare them to your own answers.

- What do you notice?

- What is your reaction? Mad, glad, sad, surprised?

- What is the most important learning point for you right now?

"There are three kinds of people in the world; those who make things happen, those who watch things happen and those who wonder what happened."

—Attributed to MARY KAY ASH

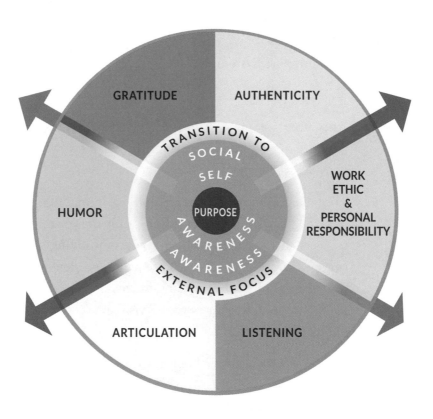

# CHAPTER 3

# CONSCIOUS SUCCESS MODEL

# 3 + 6

## SUCCESS FOUNDATION

*"You don't have to be a genius or a visionary
or even a college graduate to be successful.
You just need a framework and a dream."*
—MICHAEL DELL

THROUGHOUT THIS BOOK I STRESS THAT YOU MUST HAVE A strong sense of what your goal of "success" is. As previously mentioned, the concept of success is different for everyone. It is tied into your passion and your values. This is what makes you different.

I have had the great experience of building two homes in my life. Both were great experiences. When building a house, you have to plan, and then you can begin building from the ground up—or even below ground if you have a basement foundation. Knowing your definition of success is the blueprint of your house, your plan on which to build. You must have a visual, even if just a mental one, of what success means to you.

The foundation of a house is vitally important to the stability of the floors, walls, and roof. Equally important is the foundation of your Conscious Success Model that provides stability as you build upon your skills, talents, and goals as you journey toward achieving your vision of a successful life.

The Conscious Success Model is constructed in much the same way with two major categories or groups of "things." The first category we call the *success foundation*. In the second category are the *differentiators*. So, as the foundation of a house might contain rebar, concrete, etc., our *success foundation* contains the following three elements:

1. PURPOSE
2. SELF-AWARENESS
3. SOCIAL AWARENESS

These three elements form the foundation for defining your own success (more about that in the next chapter). It is within the confines of this deliberately built structure that you can begin creating your six differentiators.

**3 ELEMENTS**

**+**

**6 DIFFERENTIATORS**

**=**

9 DIMENSIONS OF SUCCESS!

The Conscious Success Model includes both of these two groups of ingredients—and one cannot work properly without the other:

1.  The three essential internal foundational elements:

    - Purpose

    - Self-Awareness

    - Social Awareness

2.  The six different differentiators:

    - Authenticity

    - Work Ethic and Personal Responsibility

    - Listening for Results and Connections

    - Articulate for Impact

    - Humor

    - Gratitude

The nature of growing up is learning as we go. For most, human nature and basic reinforcement prevents us from repeating mistakes, especially those with severe consequences. (Remember my waterskiing experience.) Operating your life consciously is a bit like operating machinery or driving a car— it requires concentration and the proper structure.

The issue is whether we can accelerate the process, avoid negative consequences, and also create a "discipline of consciousness" at any point in life. I submit we can, and the first step in implementing the Conscious Success Model is, in fact, building a pattern of conscious awareness on a solid foundation.

It is possible to accelerate the process and avoid negative consequences.

The three *success foundation* elements do not, by themselves, create a complete model. In Part II, I discuss in detail the six *differentiators*, which comprise the rooms within your "virtual house." Each room has a different purpose, while at the same time being part of the collective I refer to as your *conscious success*. High self-awareness links into each of the six differentiators and enhances performance in each. Think of these links or connectors as the wiring in your home. In your basement, which is part of your foundation, is a junction box. It connects your foundation to your differentiators, each needing the other to energize your house.

Most successful endeavors occur when two or more people get together and interact to produce a positive outcome. I've wracked my brain to think of occupations where no interaction occurs over a long period of time. I haven't come up with any!

Just getting by in today's world means some level of relational interactions. Beyond just getting by, thriving in today's world, especially the business world, is actually *dependent* on *effective relational interactions.*

In my field of organization development, I have worked with hundreds of organizations to improve how work is done and how results are produced more effectively. I have an organizational change management practice and methodology to help organizations implement changes on time, within budget, and meeting all the objectives. I have loads of data proving that when implementations fail, far more often than not, the *human and organizational issues are what drive failure.*

> Thriving in today's world depends on effective relational interactions.

Looking at technology implementations across many industries, the single biggest success factor has to do with humans and how well they are encouraged and reinforced to adopt new, more productive behaviors. In fact, adoption is a common success metric on technology implementations. Human behavior is at the heart of success.

Looking at history, interactions and collaboration are at the heart of the vast majority of almost all great achievements. When examining current trends and future forecasts, there is little data to suggest that human interactions will be less important moving forward. One argument can be made that they will be increasingly important—considering how the Internet is connecting more and more people worldwide every day.

## Collaboration

There is a notion that Edison was a master inventor who wore a lab coat and sat in his lab all day working alone and coming up with amazing inventions. This is far from the truth; in addition to being a great inventor, he was also a master collaborator.

Edison brought in hundreds of collaborators to help create prototypes and commercialize his inventions—people such as investors, engineers, and others to help him develop and promote the products. This led to creating more than 200 companies. In 1890, Edition established the Edison Electric Company, bringing together his various businesses.[1]

When Edison heard that Alexander Graham Bell was going to commercialize his phonograph and cylinders, Edison knew it would make his technology yesterday's news. He did not tackle this problem alone; he gathered a team, and for three days they worked on a technology that would jump over Bell's—and they succeeded.

The thing about entrepreneurs is they are fantastic at creating ideas, but they sometimes fall short by not following through and implementing the ideas. That is one of the reasons why they have to learn to collaborate with others.

> "Many ideas grow better when transplanted into another mind than in the one where they sprang up."
> —OLIVER WENDELL HOLMES SR.,
> *The Poet at the Breakfast Table*

There are many other examples in history. Consider the teams that worked on putting a man on the moon. It took hundreds of a variety of people and talents to build the craft. They needed all sorts of engineers to figure out the trajectory, communications, and more to take a team into space, fly them to the moon, land and then walk on the moon, return to the craft, fly back to Earth, and finally safely land. It required tremendous collaboration to make that happen. A great movie, *Hidden Figures,* emphasizes the critical role of three women doing very important math and technical work to support astronaut John Glenn's flight, without which the flight would not have been possible. Again, great collaboration to accomplish a common goal—a common purpose.

Now let's look at each of the Conscious Success Model's three internal elements (purpose, self-awareness, social awareness) more closely.

# SUCCESS FOUNDATION

## Purpose

In my business, I work a lot with group dynamics and group models. We work hard to get members of an organization to work collaboratively together, and we often begin with these three questions:

1. Why am I here?

2. Why are you here?

3. What result can we produce together that will create value?

These are very simple questions, yet very powerful. They begin a dialogue and create a mindset that we don't have to do everything alone, and more importantly we look for solutions to collaboration. What do each of us bring to the table? What can I expect from you? How can we produce something greater than what we could individually? Again, Ken Blanchard's great quote comes to mind, *"None of us is as smart as all of us."*

The starting point of working together is the Conscious Success Model. When we can strengthen each of these foundational elements, collaboration happens organically. Your ability to work within these foundational concepts expertly will have a huge impact on your differentiation. You will be noticed. You won't be seen as just a team player, you will be seen as a leader!

### *Living Your Life on Purpose!*

Someone once said, "The two most important days of your life are the day you are born and the day you find out why."

In Chapter 1, you were introduced to the idea of living your life on purpose. It is the idea that you are aware of your goals and how to achieve them; or, you know your destination and how you will get there. Additionally, how can you best collaborate with others?

You probably remember this conversation from *Alice's Adventures in Wonderland:*

> "Would you tell me, please, which way I ought to go from here?"
>
> "That depends a good deal on where you want to get to," said the Cat.
>
> "I don't much care where—" said Alice.

"Then it doesn't matter which way you go," said the Cat.

"—so long as I get *somewhere*," Alice added as an explanation.

"Oh, you're sure to do that," said the Cat, "if only you walk long enough."[2]

The French term *raison d'etre* means "reason for existence" or reason for being. Another way to define it would be: *"an anticipated outcome that is intended or that guides your planned actions."* I think the beauty of that definition is it contains the elements of time and action. These are both important to living out a life *on purpose!*

I have found that purpose is a critically important foundation for so many things in life. As a young boy, my father taught me about work and how to build things. Some of his important and memorable lessons dealt with learning about the purpose of various tools. Using the right tool for a job made that job much easier—using the wrong tool could ruin the job, create damage, or injure yourself.

In my years consulting and coaching with organizations, a predictable pattern in looking at high-performance organizations reveals that frequently two key documents or statements shape the organization. First, there is a clearly stated purpose or mission statement—the *what*. Second, there are defined corporate values—the *how*. So much is tied to having these aspects identified and communicated. Most excellent organizations spend a fair bit of time on these two ingredients during employee orientation or the onboarding process.

Just think about how any entity could operate effectively or perform at a high level *without* purpose and values or when these things are unclear to the members. That is a recipe for chaos at the very least. Usually the vagueness results in mis-alignment and low trust. The real cost of that dynamic is that organizations cannot move as fast as necessary, often leading to becoming non-competitive. *Alignment and speed* are great assets in business and beneficial for individuals as well.

Let's look at this first element of the model on two levels—*self-purpose* and *organizational purpose.* It should be clear what the important connection is between these two.

### *Self-Purpose*

There are often two ways people think about life and their place within it. Some feel that they are tossed about as victims of fate and they are not in control—rather, there is an *external locus of control.* This means that when bad things hap-pen, these people believe it's someone else's fault. People don't like them, things are unfair, and no matter how hard they try, others have it in for them. They're victims; they have a self-defeating attitude.

The second group believes in self-determinism. They believe that they create their own reality, and what happens to them is in their control, not someone else's. Those with an *internal locus of control* have a distinct advantage over those who believe others control their destiny. This leads to higher grades in school, and in the workplace they tend to be better at their jobs and report greater job satisfaction. Their success is not con-tingent on whether they really have more control in their lives; it is their perception that they have more control that counts.

## Perception of control counts!

How can someone shift their perception to a more internal sense of control? Start with answering this question: *"What is your purpose in life?"* This is something you really should think about carefully. Having a purpose statement as a guide helps you in a number of ways—you will become more confident, self-aware, satisfied, and determined. You may want to write down your Personal Purpose Statement (PPS) and live with it for a week or so, trying it on, before sharing it with someone you trust for reactions. However you go about this process, I predict that within a few weeks of adopting the role as your very own, you confirm and lock down your purpose.

At that point, you can appropriately, at the right time, share it with others. Going public with your purpose makes it real. It also puts the onus on you to make conscious choices to support your purpose. It's a feeling that you will enjoy—knowing why you are who you are.

Some general guidelines when writing a purpose statement:

■ Clear—easy for you and others to understand

■ Concise—simple is better, less is more, easy for you to memorize

■ Powerful and inspiring—motivates you to succeed

■ Descriptive and specific—reveals why and how you are living on purpose

As alluded to earlier, I didn't think at all about my purpose in life when I was in my 30s. I was just *doing!* My career was not very purposeful or deliberate. I did focus on next steps, but just those that were a promotion. I was chasing positions. I did all right, but again, I think it was easier back then. Job markets were not as tight, and my employer was growing rapidly at that time.

I wish I had spent time at least thinking about and determining my life's purpose. I could have more thoughtfully and consciously aligned my actions and decisions with my purpose for much better results. I certainly could have done it more efficiently. Today, there is less margin for error or tolerance for wasted motion.

Being clear on your purpose has huge benefits. Once you have a clear purpose, you can:

- Set annual and long-range goals to achieve your purpose.

- Consider what your ongoing development plan needs to be to achieve your purpose with continuous improvement. For example, what training and education should you pursue?

- Evaluate how you show up in life—are you living out your purpose? Look at decisions, actions, and behaviors to see if they are all consistent with your purpose.

It is important to remember, just as the mission of organizations can change over time requiring updating, so too you should revisit your PPS every few years for alignment or update.

*A Second Consideration*

Considering your organizational purpose ensures that you're in the right kind of organization *for you!*

As with my starting example, most corporate organizations have some sort of stated vision or mission statement. Most also identify a set of values as well. You can make better career choices and operate with higher awareness if you consciously compare your PPS and values with those of the organization you might be interested in joining. If you are currently employed with a company, check your PPS with the purpose of your company and compare the values. If you find there is some misalignment, it's worth thinking about. It would not necessarily mean you should leave that company, but you certainly might find it is much harder work to remain. If the misalignment is severe, it really is worth evaluating your continued fit.

# Self-Awareness

Patrick Lencioni wrote in the Foreword of the book *Emotional Intelligence 2.0*:

> Not education. Not experience. Not knowledge or intellectual horsepower. None of these serve as an adequate predictor as to why one person succeeds and another doesn't. There is something else going on that society doesn't seem to account for.[3]

I believe that "something else" is self-awareness.

When the film *Animal House* was released in 1978, some of my closest friends from college were convinced it was a "documentary" based on their real fraternity experiences. As entertainment, it contains many funny scenes, lines, and some great performances by popular actors of the day. I've always thought it was a very funny film and it certainly highlights many elements of college-level humor and bad behavior for that time. That's clearly part of the "funny factor." It's designed to entertain, not to be a model for young people to follow. That said, the film can teach a lesson about the consequences of stumbling through life in a totally carefree, reactive manner (notwithstanding the humorous futures identified for the key characters at the conclusion of the movie, especially Bluto, John Belushi's character).

The characters didn't seem to demonstrate a very conscious intent with high awareness. The characters were not unconscious (except maybe after the toga party), but they certainly were not totally conscious either. Being clear about the various consequences of their choices was not much of a priority. I have to say I probably operated similarly at times when I was that age.

My simple definition of *self-awareness* is having the capacity for introspection and knowing at any point in time what is going on with you. It means you can see yourself as separate from others and the environment and can focus on your thoughts, feelings, physical state, and belief systems. This capacity or ability creates the solid foundation for much of life.

As my mentor John Jones used to say, *"Awareness precedes meaningful choice."* From an early age, making good choices is a big part of life. It's near impossible to make great choices with no self-awareness. As someone who has been in the business of helping others with their own development for many years, I can say that it truly *is* impossible to improve yourself without self-awareness.

I was recently coaching a very senior executive of a large pharmaceutical company. In the course of talking with her, we discussed a meeting she had with another executive. The meeting had not gone as well as my client had hoped. We discussed the dynamics—what could have made the outcome better, what was the root cause. I asked whether the other individual was under any type of stress or pressure and my client said that yes, she suspected the other individual was under a lot of pressure and clearly not in the best space. My coaching then took the direction of how my client could be more supportive of this other individual as this is a pattern. The real point of this example is to highlight how interactions are compromised when one or both parties are not at their best. What could be, hopefully should be, a good outcome in any interaction, can head south in a hurry when we are not at our best; or the other person is not at his or her best.

> It is impossible to improve yourself without self-awareness.

I think true self-awareness is in somewhat short supply today, yet it doesn't have to be that way. Two major aspects of life contribute to this shortage: 1. lack of knowledge and a structure to raise your own self-awareness; and 2. the rush, stress, and pressure of everyday life.

Some really great information on self-awareness can be found in the book *Emotional Intelligence 2.0* by

Travis Bradberry and Jean Greaves. There is a close connection between self-awareness and emotional intelligence. They even offer an assessment when you buy the book.[4] The following is a fun graphic of different emotional states.

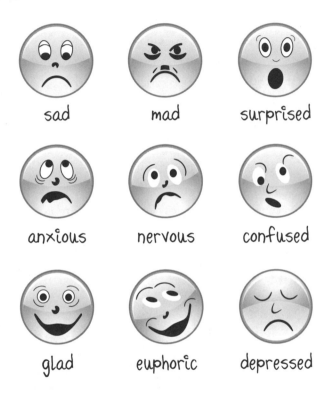

You can use these expressions to determine how you are feeling about a particular situation. Be aware of your mental and emotional state at all times. Take a moment right now and pick the image that best describes your current mood. Hopefully you are fairly relaxed as you are reading. Sometimes you may want to "check into" yourself. If you know you're stressed or upset, you may want to wait before "assessing" or making any important decisions. Honestly, taking time to reflect is always your best option, rather than responding at the moment of intense emotion.

Many people do not like pauses or silences. We feel compelled to fill them. Notice when you are in this situation. Sometimes it feels awkward, but taking the time necessary to say the right thing takes…well, time. You can say that you need some time to reflect and think on a particular subject. People will understand.

Those who choose their words wisely and make smart decisions have a great deal of differentiation; they are seen as distinct. They truly listen to what others are saying and they value their position enough to reflect and respond only when they have the most appropriate answer.

The best way to express what is going on is completing the following two sentences:

- Right now I'm thinking…

- Right now I'm feeling…

Your answers give a clear indication of what is going on inside you and communicate your given state and thoughts on a particular subject.

If you are clear on your purpose, then it's important to know how you are feeling and even what your physical state is. If you are feeling angry or sick, your performance will be affected. If you are afraid or stressed, then obviously your best work will not come forward. Being constantly aware of your inner state maximizes your ability to operate on purpose.

### Get Some Sleep

One time I was working with a company with change-management issues. I thought I was doing a solid job for the company until one of the senior executives approached me in the hall and said, "Listen, David, I only have a minute, but I needed to ask you a favor. I need your help convincing the senior leaders about the value of the work you are doing, the value of change management for the company, and why we are investing in it. I'm sorry I don't have more time to discuss it, but I'm rushing off to a meeting right now. We can talk about it more later."

She rushed off to her meeting before I could really respond, and I didn't see her the rest of the day. A deadly seed of doubt had been planted within me. I went back to my hotel room that night deflated. I thought, *They don't think I'm doing a good job…that what I'm offering the company doesn't have value.* I knew better, but I took it personally. I was afraid my time with them was coming to an abrupt end.

The doubt triggered my insecurities, and because I had low self-awareness I was not in touch with what was happening and what the potential impact was going to be. I tossed and turned all night, extremely stressed about what was going to happen— and what I could do about it.

The next morning I had a presentation to give to a group. I knew the material backward and forward, and all of my materials were prepared. I was tired, stressed, and insecure and did not have the awareness to predict what would happen next.

I gave the presentation and received a lukewarm response. I was asked questions that I did not answer very well. I was totally off my game. In fact, one of my colleagues noticed and asked me what was wrong after the meeting. My low self-awareness had a negative impact, not only on my presentation but also on my purpose of delivering excellent material, content, and support to the company.

### The Rest of the Story

I had to clear the air, so I found the senior executive who had approached me.

"Listen, I need more clarification on what you need from me to help you relay the value of what I'm doing."

"David, we all think you're doing a fantastic job. We all can see the changes within the organization. The trouble I'm having is clearly articulating those changes to the rest of the team. I just need your help in the proper language and examples of your work."

Oh! I had gone straight to the dark side. As my wife puts it, I had a "disaster fantasy." Sometimes parents have these dark thoughts if they don't see their child for a period of time and immediately go to thinking something terrible has happened to the child.

Having a strong self-awareness will filter out these disaster fantasies because we are more aware of our feelings, thoughts, and triggers. When we begin to feel something is amiss, with self-awareness we can begin to ask questions, seek clarification, and assume the best based on our skill sets and abilities.

Colin Powell, in his book *It Worked for Me,* talks about a number of techniques he learned. One is "Wait till tomorrow." A new day, a new dawn will often have you seeing things in better light. A good night's sleep is important to a good day's work. To transition from Self Awareness to Social Awareness, here is a fun story which touches both dimensions.

A good friend of mine and his wife have a beautiful, exceptionally bright daughter named McKenna attending the University of Colorado.

A few years ago, before McKenna got into CU, my friend was expressing frustration about some of her habits living at home. "Dave, it drives me crazy that she leaves her K-Cup after using the Keurig, and after eating cereal, she leaves the bowl and spoon in the sink when the dishwasher is a foot away!"

Years later, McKenna started college at CU. On one of her weekends at home, she and my friend were discussing the college experience and apartment life with roommates. McKenna expressed her frustration at her roommates leaving dirty dishes in the sink when "the dishwasher is LITERALLY right next to the sink."

My friend smiled and said, "Wow, that must be frustrating! That situation seems familiar to me—even more familiar, right here in our own kitchen." McKenna and my friend had a laugh, and the story illustrates how if we pay attention, the behaviors of *others* can help *us* become more self aware and socially aware.

## Social Awareness

Very simply, *social awareness* is knowing what the impact on others is when you do or say something. It is being conscious of your impact on others as you travel through life.

As part of my executive coaching practice, I use a simple *impact vs. intent* model. In your interaction with others, does your *impact* match your *intent?* This is a great silent conversation for you to have as you interact with others. Even better, it's a good question for you to ask *before* you have an interaction with someone else. It is particularly important for you to check your intent before what you feel might be a difficult conversation. Specifically, it helps to train yourself to take a moment before *doing* or *saying* anything to reflect on, "What is my desired result here? What is my intent?"

Does what you say or do with others have the desired results? Does it produce the results that are in sync with your purpose? This is where collaboration is important and these three questions are most applicable:

1. Why am I here?

2. Why are you here?

3. What result can we produce together which will create value?

This again means having an ongoing awareness. In addition to looking inward, we have to also be aware of our outward impact.

The starting point is that you have to care about how others are affected by your words and actions. I think most people do care. Your upbringing probably included lessons from your parents on being polite and considerate of others. As children, you might have been told these behaviors were "good manners." As adults and professionals in any field, this quality goes beyond just good manners and focuses on producing respectful, effective relationships for the good of a larger effort.

### Narcissism

Recently, we were working with an organization where the executive team was attempting to roll out major changes within the organization. The CEO was having trouble collaborating because of the way she was interfacing with others on the executive team.

During meetings, she dominated the conversations and was very critical and autocratic. She was directive to the point of being dictatorial. She wanted to be noticed as the most important person in the room, if not the smartest person in the room. She was not aware of her negative impact on the team. Her behavior and communication style screamed insecurity and domination, which prevented the team from wanting to participate. If she had a greater *social* awareness she would have realized that her purpose of creating change was being thwarted by her low *self*-awareness.

She is now working on increasing self-awareness and realizes that her behavior impacts her purpose and the purpose of the executive team. It is a work in progress, but she seeks every day to be more aware of the impact of her words and emotional state when she walks into meetings with her team. You've heard of the Golden Rule: "Treat others as you would like to be treated." Personally, I think the "Platinum Rule" is better: "Treat others as *they would like to be treated.*" When you can consciously operate that way, you are at the height of social awareness.

Here are a few questions to ask yourself to remove the blind spots in your relations:

1. Was I attentive to the person who approached me?

2. Did I blow the person off because I was too busy to listen?

3. Was I diligent in asking questions about the content of what the person said? Was I attentive to the person's feelings and emotions?

4. What was my body language, facial expression, and voice tone? How did these impact the other person?

### *Assessment: Three Foundational Elements*

Do a quick self-assessment on how you see your current performance considering the three foundational elements. Use a three-point scale where:

1. = Currently undeveloped

2. = Underdeveloped, improvement wanted

3. = I'm satisfied with my current level of development.

Purpose: _____

Self-Awareness: ____ _____

Social Awareness: _____

# Now What?

1. Create a *Personal Purpose Statement (PPS)*. Spend time really thinking about your purpose and how it relates to all aspects of your life. Share your statement with a few trusted others to elicit constructive feedback.

2. Begin to work on your self-awareness as defined in this chapter. Ask yourself the three questions and make it a regular check-in routine at least once a day.

   ▪ What am I thinking?

- What am I feeling?

- What is my impact on others?

3.  Use the following questions to assess your level of social awareness:

    - What is my intent in a particular interaction?

    - Did my impact match my intent?

    - How do I know?

    - Did I check in with the other individual?

    - Am I creating the quality of interaction that I desire with another individual?

4.  Another helpful technique is to regularly check in with people you interact with to see if your impact is matching your intent. That can be accomplished by asking the simple question, "In this recent situation, my intent was to _____. How did I do in your opinion?"

In the next chapter you will read about the concept of differentiation. It is what we do or say that catches people's attention. It sets us apart from the rest. It doesn't mean we exist outside of a group; rather, it helps us define our role and importance as a leader and part of a greater team to others.

> "Everything that irritates us about others can
> lead us to an understanding of ourselves."
> —CARL JUNG, *Memories, Dreams, Reflections*

# CHAPTER 4

# DIFFERENTIATION AND SHOWING UP

*"It wasn't that Microsoft was so brilliant or clever in copying the Mac, it's just that the Mac was a sitting duck for 10 years. That's Apple's problem: Their differentiation evaporated."*
—STEVE JOBS, *Apple Confidential 2.0*

I LIVE IN THE MOUNTAINS OF COLORADO AT ABOUT EIGHT thousand feet in elevation. When it snows in Colorado, it really snows. There is nothing like looking out the window and seeing a world blanketed in snow. When it's really deep, everything has a smooth, shapeless quality. Unless you know what lies beneath, it all looks the same.

I have always been told that each snowflake is unique. The crystalline structure forms in different patterns each time the water vapor freezes in the atmosphere. With the naked eye, the snowflakes look like one big, fluffy white blanket covering roads and pavements, fields and trees. It takes a microscope to see each crystalline structure clearly.

Likewise, each of us is unique in our make-up, but we can all seem the same from a distance. Sometimes the distance is being part of a large organization or a group. We become part of an unremarkable landscape. How can you stand out? How can you entice someone to look at you close enough to see your uniqueness?

This is not about vanity or pride, it's about necessity. As Charles Darwin wrote, "Intelligence is based on how efficient a species became at doing the things they need to survive." I paraphrase that and say, "Awareness, or consciousness, ensures how a species will do the things needed to thrive."

Like the theory of *survival of the fittest,* your road to success (however you define that) may be more about choices you make that link *consciously* to your success. As you have already read, the cards can be stacked against you; consequently, you need to be conscious about where you stand among your peers. We cannot float around like some ubiquitous snowflakes, relying on fate to be noticed. You have to be more proactive, more deliberate and consciously aware. This *is* conscious success.

## Survey Data Analysis

**Question 1**: Think of one or two very successful (in business and life) individuals you've witnessed/admired in your career. What two or three questions or personality traits in those successful individuals do you believe most contributed to their success?

What was it that made the people in the survey think about those one or two individuals? They had *differentiation*. They were purple snowflakes in a shower of white. Something stood out and made them notice and remember that particular individual.

At the end of Chapter 3, I encouraged you to answer Question 1 yourself. What was it about your choices that stood out? Could you picture the one or two people in your mind? Could you hear their voices? Was there a particular phrase they used? Did they wear unusual clothes?

Differentiation can come in many forms. The trick, of course, is to be noticed for the right reasons. You don't want to differentiate yourself in a way that hinders rather than helps you. For example, if you arrive late to work, tell off-color jokes, or frequently wear wrinkled clothes, you will be noticed. Each of those are differentiators, but not good ones.

In this book, we focus on the positive differentiators, but you might also want to think about the negative ones and how to eliminate them. Recognizing warts is part of self-awareness. When you see one, you should take steps to remove it. Each of the differentiators provides ways to do just that. But it all begins with a strong self-awareness.

## Mind Your Five Ps and "Cues"

I realize that you may not have a background in marketing, so I'm going to give you a quick Marketing 101 rundown. If you're a marketer, you can skip this next part and I will rejoin you for beer in the next section.

When you are bringing a product to market, there are "Five Ps of Marketing." These key rules, when considered and followed, increase the salability, or marketability, of your product:

1.  **Product**. What pain or need does the product solve for the customer? In addition, the product must be easy to use, visually appealing, and have great packaging. Without a great product, the other four Ps will not really matter. Presentation is key.

2.  **Place**. Where is your product located? Is it easily seen? Is it placed in the right market and stores? Not having the right placement of a product can doom it to fail, no matter how wonderful it might be. Proper placement is key.

3.  **Promotion**. Without having the right promotion to attract your customers, you will not sell your product. It could be in the right place and be a great product, but no one has never heard of it or isn't looking for it. Active promoting is key.

4.  **Price**. Your product must be priced to sell. This does not mean it is eternally discounted. When you're pricing a product, you must know four things: 1. your cost to produce it, 2. what the competition is charging, 3. what is the standard markup or profit margin in your particular industry, and 4. what value it has to the customer. Consider the question, "What will it cost the customer to *not* buy my product?" Value to others is key.

5. **Profit**. Without profit, you don't have a business. It is the space between your price and what it costs you to produce. (This is an oversimplification, because cost refers to more than material costs.) As mentioned in number 4, you need to know what the profit margin is for your particular industry and set that as your goal. Your price and your product have to be in alignment to achieve the profit margin you're after. Perceived gain is key.

# Beer

Okay, so now that all of the savvy marketing people have joined us again, let's talk about beer. For many years I worked for a large beverage company, and we worked hard to differentiate our products in the market. Here is how the Five Ps aligned for us.

1. **Product**. I can honestly say we produced a great beer, but let's be honest—there are a lot of different beers to choose from. We had been brewing our beer the same way for generations, so we looked at the product in a different way. People wanted an excellent beer, we knew that, so we added something that became a new standard. We advertised that our beer was cold-brewed and told people this made a superior beer. In fact, we colored the packaging silver and added mountains to make it look cold. Everything screamed ice-cold beer. Cold-brewed, cold-served, and cold going down. People don't like hot beer, so

this was, in short, genius. People noticed, and at that time we cornered the market.

2.   **Placement**. Location is so important for beer and many other food items in stores. The more visible a beer is, the more people gravitate toward it. That meant we wanted premium shelf placement, prominent displays of beer cases that customers would have to navigate around, and displays that shouted at the consumer, "BUY ME FOR YOUR SUPERBOWL, PICNIC, AND PARTIES. YOUR EVENT WON'T BE COMPLETE WITHOUT OUR BEER." We wanted our product visible and well-stocked. This, of course, costs money, but placement is very important in differentiation. Distribution is key.

3.   **Promotion**. Promotion includes television, print media, and events. We had full teams of people working on promotion, not only for media but also promotions in stores. We had contests, giveaways, and sales. All of these to catch the eyes of customers and get them to buy a case of beer, even if they had entered the store with the intention of buying only cat food.

4.   **Price**. Price fluctuates all the time. We had to be competitive with our market, cover our costs, and make a decent profit margin. At times we dropped our prices for certain promotions, but these were done strategically. The pricing and value relationship is key.

5.  **Profit**. We had a great product, a great strategic plan of promoting and selling, and we had a competitive price in the market. Profits went up and down, but we stayed within our target margin over time. We had a vision of what our profit would be, and everything else we did was in pursuit of that. If we needed a new line of beers, a new slogan, or a new design, all of these were driven by the idea that whatever we invested, we would make back and hit our profit margin.

## The Five Ps of You

What does all this mean to you? We have already established that you're not a snowflake, and I can confidently say that you're not a can a beer. But in the job market, you *are* a commodity that you are trying to sell. You are the product and the company trying to sell the product. Like any other product, you should consider your own Five Ps. How are you selling yourself? How are you differentiating yourself? How do you stand out in a pool of applicants for one position?

When people are looking for beer for a particular event and all of the beer looks and appears the same, they will often go to the brands they know, and those with the competitive price. In the job market, the same is true. Unless someone really stands out, employers will often choose those they know and whose value is clear.

Let's break down your personal Five Ps. These are your personal keys to conscious success in the job market.

1.  **Presentation**. What package are you presenting? There are two areas to consider. First is your

resume. Is it up to date? Does it look professional, or is it a boring template? Does it have spelling and grammar errors? Do you jump off the page and grab the person reading it?

The second part is the physical package. I realize that every job market has a certain uniform. Whether it is a suit or a police uniform, there are rules that apply. How you appear creates an impression on others—both positively and negatively. You can argue that it should not matter, but you may be having that argument in the unemployment line.

Cleanliness is vitally important. Personal hygiene should not have to be discussed, but I will anyway. Groomed hair, clean fingernails, and free of odor are the basics. Free of odor includes not only perspiration odor but also overpowering perfume and aftershave odor.

You can't make a second first impression, so put your best foot forward the first time. You want the entire package to make others think you are professional. Sloppy and smelly are differentiators, but not good ones.

2. **Proper placement**. How are you placing yourself in the market? Is the job you have currently going to put you into the position you want in the future? Do you have the necessary skills and education to leverage yourself? These are just some of the questions you should be asking yourself. You need to be seen and perceived

as the perfect person for the position you desire. You will learn about conscious awareness in the following chapters to truly look at where you are in relation to where you want to go.

3. **Active promoting**. Networking properly is a skill to learn. You don't want to come on too strong, but on the other hand you don't want to be a wallflower. Seek opportunities to meet and connect with people. Remember, when leaders need someone to fill a position, they will consider those they know and are familiar with first. You will learn how to be more effective in connecting with others when we discuss success differentiators.

4. **Profit/value**. What value do you offer to others? To your company? To your department? Knowing your value is something we will unpack further because it relates to how you are presenting yourself. It is also important when considering your salary. How much are your time and skills worth? In order to project that to others, you must know what it is yourself. You don't want to overrate yourself or you could price yourself out of the running. You don't want to underrate yourself, having people perceive you are of less value or, worse, leave money on the table. Talk about the price and value relationship with your boss or the person interviewing you.

5. **Perceived gain**. What will people gain by working with you? This is not always about what *you* will gain; if you start off with that, you could turn off others to your real worth. If you want a position or a contract, you want those considering you to perceive not only your value, but why you are the best choice.

# Don't Leave It to Fate

Can you imagine how long we would have been in business if we had the attitude, "We have a good tasting beer. People will share it, probably, and then everyone will want to buy it."

Sounds ridiculous, right? Then why would people have the goal, "If I graduate college and work hard, people will notice me and eventually I will rise to the top."

To stand out, you must be deliberate in your strategy. You must have *purposeful differentiation*. You must actively work on your key differentiators. I mean a "look at them, write them down, post them on the bathroom mirror" kind of strategy. Everything you do should have the purpose of achieving the goals you set for yourself. For example, this goal includes factors that have to be accomplished to achieve the goal: "I want to be VP of sales in five years. I need two certifications, and I need to be in a management position in the next two years to even be considered."

You will learn about the Consciousness Success Model in the next chapter and begin to bring into focus your strategy for change and differentiation.

# Impact Must Equal Intent

> "Nothing of me is original. I am the combined
> effort of everyone I've ever known."
> —CHUCK PALAHNIUK, *Invisible Monsters*

My time growing up was fairly typical. My father worked for United Airlines in a variety of executive positions, rising up to becoming the assistant to the president. My mother was a homemaker and took care of three kids, two dogs, and one parakeet. Hard to say who had the tougher job, but I'd bet on my mom.

Both Mom and Dad were part of the "Greatest Generation," having survived the Great Depression (1929–39). My dad was in the Army Air Corps during World War II. These nation and world events are significant because they shaped who they became and what they imparted to my sisters and me, which directly affected every success I've had in life.

Both of my parents took their roles seriously, shaping their kids to be independent, productive individuals. Like many parents and especially those of that generation, my folks clearly wanted a better life for their kids than what they had experienced growing up through the depression and war years.

One of the most powerful lessons my dad taught me was *how to show up in life*. I remember at a very early age, maybe six or seven, he began teaching me how to introduce myself. He lovingly but firmly told me, "When you meet someone, look them in the eye and shake their hand with a firm handshake— and with a clear, strong voice, tell them your name."

I've never forgotten that advice, and it's served me well. How you introduce yourself is the start of how people experience you. We've all heard the expression "You only get one chance at a first impression." It's a pretty good idea to make that first impression a good one.

> Whatever you choose to do in life,
> do it the very best way possible.

Another important lesson espoused by Mother and Father was that it doesn't matter what you choose to do in life; but whatever you choose, try and do it the very best way possible. All of us kids started working at an early age.

The point is that I was fortunate to have a great influence from my parents about basic behaviors (how to "show up" in life), work, and a work ethic. To some degree today that is also true, but with both parents working in most families that influence is more of a challenge due to time constraints.

What I have learned through my success and through the interviews was how important the concept of how you "show up" truly is. How you show up, how you present yourself, is related to the impact you will make.

Some people mistake intent for impact. We want to make a great impression and stand out in the most positive light. The challenge is that your actual impact, based on how you show up, may not match your intent.

If you show up as a mess (I use this term to mean many aspects of your life) but want to impress people, your impact will surely fall short of your intent.

So, ask yourself: *How am I really showing up? How am I presenting myself to others? Am I having the impact I really want to make?*

After taking time to thoughtfully complete the Now What? section, in the next few chapters we examine the six differentiators that will make a huge impact on your future success.

## Now What?

Utilize the knowledge about yourself to consciously think through some questions such as:

- How am I too similar to others in ways that cause me to get lost in the crowd?

- What are my positive differentiations?

- What are the five to seven things that cause me to be memorable and more consciously successful?

- What are my Five Ps and how can I begin to improve them?

> "You have to do things right to stay in business, and that's not easy, and that's a choice on a daily basis, the choices you make in how to run your business and how to have a point of differentiation and how to be true to your brand, how to offer something that people want and to offer something that you love."
>
> —VENUS WILLIAMS,
> *Professional tennis player*

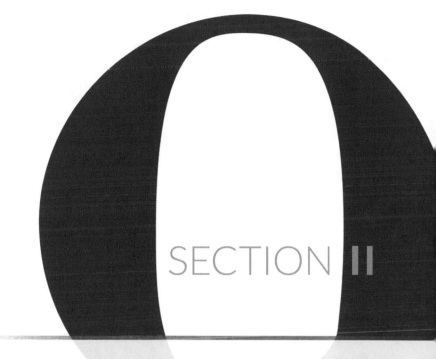

SECTION **II**

# DIFFERENTIATORS

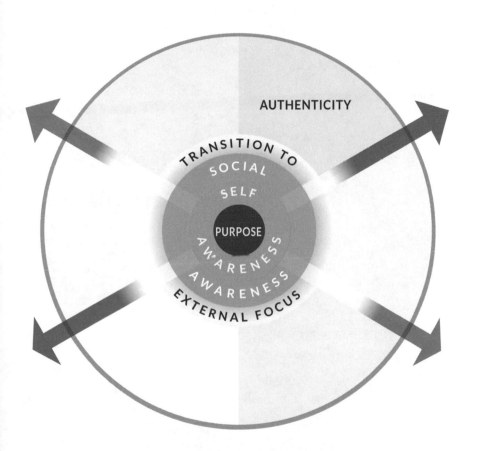

AUTHENTICITY

TRANSITION TO

SOCIAL

SELF

PURPOSE

AWARENESS

AWARENESS

EXTERNAL FOCUS

# DIFFERENTIATOR 1—
# AUTHENTICITY

# CHAPTER 5

# AUTHENTICITY

*"Be yourself. Everyone else is already taken."*
—ANONYMOUS

---

**AUTHENTICITY**—Never deceiving yourself
or others in how you show up.

---

AT THE END OF CHAPTER 2, I HAD CONCLUDED THAT TWELVE common themes had emerged from the answers from my survey:

- Purpose
- Belief Systems and Values
- Social Awareness
- Application and Implementation
- Communication and Listening

- Leadership and Mentorship

- Flexibility

- Humility

- Knowledge

- Self-Awareness

- Support System

- Independence

I spent some time contemplating these categories and put them through the filter of my own life and experience. Three of these should jump right out as the three foundational elements of the Conscious Success Model—purpose, self-awareness, social awareness. I was left with nine others to consider, and how they related to conscious success. I found some were similar, and a new pattern emerged.

As discussed in Chapter 4, a major theme of this book is how to differentiate ourselves. When I reread the answers to the interview questions, certain differentiators became evident when people discussed what stood out to them about people who were successful as well as what helps them stand out and be successful. Six differentiators emerged:

1.  Be authentic.

2.  Demonstrate a solid work ethic and personal responsibility.

3.  Listen for results and connection.

4.  Articulate for impact.

5.  See and demonstrate humor.

6.  Demonstrate gratitude.

For each of the six differentiators, I connect them to the Conscious Success Model, as each must be in alignment with the three core principles—purpose, self-awareness, and social awareness.

When these differentiators are used in conjunction with the *success foundation,* the chances of differentiating yourself are multiplied exponentially. This is the secret sauce to *conscious success.*

Someone once said, "Be yourself. Everyone else is already taken." It seems obvious and simple—just be yourself. Authenticity is the first differentiator, and I chose it for a reason. Without authenticity, the rest of the differentiators will not matter. You cannot differentiate yourself based on a false image of yourself. You have to be true to your image, and your image must be true to who you are.

Consider our quote again. It seems like a fundamental concept, and everyone who reads it says, "Of course I'm being myself. That's silly!"

Yet we have all encountered people who are not truly authentic in their day-to-day lives. Let's test this idea with a quick exercise. You'll need a piece of paper and a writing implement. Follow these steps in order:

1.  Draw a line down the middle of the page.

2.  Think of one (no more than two) person(s) you know who you would say is truly authentic—*real!* When you're around the person you

experience "WYSIWYG" (what you see is what you get). Okay, do you have someone in mind? Write the name at the top left side of the page.

3. Under the person's name, write some words that describe the person.

4. Now under this first set of words, write down what the experience is like when you spend time with this person. How do you *feel* after you spent time with this person?

5 Now think of someone you know who is not authentic, someone who projects a certain phoniness. Okay, do you have someone in mind? Write the name at the top of the right side of the page.

6. Below the name, describe this person.

7. Under the set of descriptive words, write what the experience is like when you spend time with this person. How do you *feel* after spending time with this person?

8. Now compare the two sides of the page. What do you notice?

When I do this exercise with folks, it is not surprising that the descriptions of the two people are very different. The descriptors are far less complimentary for the person thought of as a phony, inauthentic. In other words, lack of authenticity colors the way we think of these people. Also not surprising, it is more work being around inauthentic people and generally not very enjoyable.

Part of the purpose of that exercise is to raise your awareness. You may be a very authentic person. If not, be aware of the consequences; others will notice if you are not living and operating as authentically as possible.

After doing the exercise, do one final iteration of the exercise. Put *your* name at the top of a different sheet of paper. Now write down, below your name, five to seven descriptive words that describe how you *want* others to see you when you are completely authentic. This can serve as a guideline for you in your day-to-day dealings with others.

## Two Sides of Authenticity

Let me be clear on the idea of differentiators, as this is true of all of them. Each of the six differentiators contain two sides of the same coin. The more extreme you are on each side of the coin, the more you will be noticed. Let me use authenticity as an example. If you are truly authentic in everything you say and do, people will trust you, look up to you, and want to be close to you. They will know when they ask you a question, you will return to them an authentic, honest answer.

So the flip side of this authenticity duality is being inauthentic. People quickly notice when others are being fake. Just look at your answers in the exercise. You identified one—and I'm sure you can think of others. We don't trust people who are not authentic. Words such as *fraudulent, fake,* and *hypocrite* are associated with this type of person. They have definitely differentiated themselves, but in a way that says, "Don't trust me. Stay away from me because I'm unpredictable in my responses. You will never really know me."

> Consistency is the key of all
> the differentiators.

We will explore this duality for each differentiator because no one wants to be noticed for the wrong reasons. Sometimes we can be challenged and slip, but that is not what people watch the closest. We all are guilty of being inauthentic because we all have a bad day now and then. What people want to know is how you will recover from those times.

Consistency is the key of all the differentiators. When we are consistently authentic and all of a sudden we are not, it does not change people's opinions unless it is severe. They may just chalk it up to a bad day or that we had a reason to act differently, because they know we are consistently a particular way.

Major inconsistencies cannot be ignored, so it is very important to have a strong foundation, a strong sense of purpose.

## Being Authentic Takes Work

When I was younger, my grandfather always told me, "Tell the truth; that way you don't have to remember what you said."

It is so much easier to remember the truth. You don't have to worry about getting caught up in a lie or tell another lie to cover it. When you are truthful with everything you say, you build your credibility and reduce your stress.

I work hard to be authentic. It's easier now; I have less to prove because people know I'm authentic. That said, I can certainly remember a lot of times when I was younger when I was clearly not operating with authenticity. In focusing on this important element, I take my definition from a great mentor of mine, John Jones, who taught me, *"I never want to deceive myself or others."*

The quote is elegant in its simplicity. It's easy to say and harder to do. If we're going to be successful with this element, it really must start with a clear sense of purpose and a high level of self-awareness. That allows you to be conscious in how you operate hour to hour, day to day.

> Be true to yourself.

It follows that being true to yourself is much easier if you've defined what that means, what that might look like to others. This is where your personal purpose statement kicks in. It provides you with a standard against which you measure yourself.

There are many reasons why we might not be totally true to ourselves. One of the most common I've witnessed is the belief that if we portray ourselves as something other than who we really are, we will be seen as more desirable or popular. I think most people can think of times when we tried to project a different image.

High school and college years are often difficult times for many in terms of self-image or self-confidence. I was very insecure during those times in my life. I can remember projecting an air of self-confidence to cover up a lot of insecurities. I can also remember it may have gotten me through some tough times but ultimately caught up with me.

As a youngster I found that one way to mask my insecurities was through humor (sometimes inappropriate humor). If I could be the class clown, it might generate some approval and affection. It worked! Many from my college and high school years would probably say I was a funny guy. It's actually well documented in the field of comedy and professional comedians that many are seeking love and approval through their acts. It's quite common. There can be a price to pay, however.

I went through an intense development process to gain credentials in the field of organization development (OD). The development curriculum was necessary and taught me a lot. I remember sitting through a number of training group (t-group) sessions. T-groups were a popular technique to assist groups and individuals in raising awareness and working on issues. In a t-group, an individual often receives more direct feedback in several hours than many people get in a lifetime.

In my own experience, after about seven days of intense work (working from 7:30 A.M. until 10:00 P.M. with only bio breaks and meal breaks), I was sitting in this t-group and it was my turn to receive feedback. The common theme in the group was that individuals found me humorous but could not determine who I really was. They couldn't determine what kind of person I was. They had no sense of what was important to me. On the basis of all this, the common conclusion was that they could not trust me. I was not trustworthy. That was a pretty difficult pill to swallow. I can recall that it was not fun for me at the time—yet it was probably one of the most important experiences I've had in life.

At that point in my life I was well beyond "needing" to entertain—it was habit. I saw myself as very trustworthy and honest. I really wanted to be seen as *real* more than humorous. It was a great awakening for me to see myself through the eyes of others. It was actually great to be seen in the different light provided by the t-group feedback. Many people don't have that kind of experience and sometimes learn the price of inauthenticity the hard way.

# The Price of Inauthenticity

I was really disappointed when one of my favorite news anchors was caught being inauthentic. Brian Williams had stated that he had been in a helicopter that had received gunfire during his coverage of the Iraq war in 2003. Years later, people who were there came forward and said his story was not true; he had not been shot down in the Chinook helicopter and forced to land.

He experienced the true cost of being inauthentic as other stories of his were questioned such as his coverage of Hurricane Katrina and the Berlin Wall coming down. As a journalist, honesty, integrity, and authenticity are paramount. Once Williams lost that, he lost his job.

One of the significant consequences of not being authentic is erosion of trust. It's very hard to trust people who project something they aren't.

# Trust

Let's look at the trust issue on a tactical level, and at a very specific tool to increase your trustworthiness and, by extension, your authenticity.

There are some good books and articles on trust and undoubtedly some good definitions. I like to keep it simple. For me, trust between two or more people is simply "expectations met or unmet." Generally, if you repeatedly do what you say you will do, others will find you to be *trustworthy*. The opposite is also true.

Years ago, I learned about a simple model called "**Management by Agreement—MBA**" taught to me by great mentors at The Atlanta Consulting Group. Basically, it is a trust model for making and keeping agreements.

The model has four basic tips or practices:

1. Make only agreements you intend to keep.

2. Avoid making or accepting fuzzy agreements.

3. If you have to break an agreement in the future, give earliest possible notice.

4. If you break an agreement, clean it up immediately.

If you have mastered the clarity of your purpose and you operate with high self-awareness, you then can become effective and impactful when you are operating *authentically!*

When you are living your life on purpose, you are living your authentic life. Everything you do has a purpose. No longer do you have to walk the road of being the victim or victor of chance. *You* are making the rules and *you* are living by them every day.

Consider what you post on social media. We will talk more about your impact in the way you express yourself, but for now consider how consistent your posts are with how you represent yourself offline. If there is a huge difference, this can cause brand confusion. Which is the authentic you? The one online or offline? How authentic are you if you are inconsistent in your messages?

Many employers are aware of this conundrum and often look at a candidate's online presence as a factor in the hiring practice. If the person appears to be great on paper and had a great interview but posts outrageous pictures and comments online, the person could be passed over.

## Now What?

1. Assess key points (assessment items) where you generally see yourself (or how others see you) in terms of being inauthentic and authentic.

2. Create an action plan to close the gap.

3. Make **management by agreement** a standard part of how you operate with people.

"I never wanted to be like somebody. I wanted to be the first me, not the next somebody else."
—DANICA PATRICK

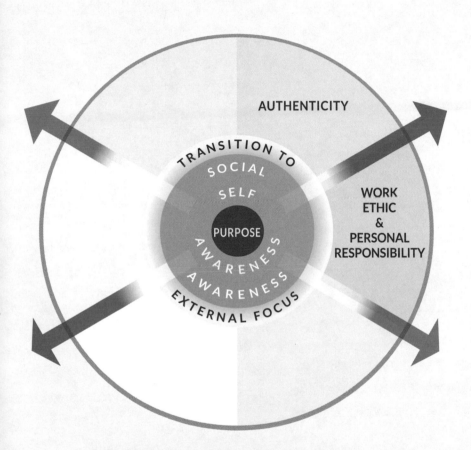

# DIFFERENTIATOR 2—
# WORK ETHIC AND PERSONAL
# RESPONSIBILITY

# CHAPTER 6

# WORK ETHIC AND PERSONAL RESPONSIBILITY

*"Talent is cheaper than table salt. What separates the talented individual from the successful one is a lot of hard work."*
—STEPHEN KING

---

WORK ETHIC AND PERSONAL RESPONSIBILITY—Work with conviction to produce the results you desire and take responsibility for the results produced— even when they fail to meet the desired result.

---

THERE IS FREQUENTLY INTERESTING CONFUSION SURROUNDING the correlation of effort and result. Some people equate time invested (effort) with increased productivity. Is that a valid connection? Not necessarily—consider the information presented in the following table.

| Most Productive Countries, 2015[1] | | | | | |
|---|---|---|---|---|---|
| Rank | Country | GDP per hour worked | Employed Population | GDP (USD) | Average work week (hrs) |
| 1 | Luxembourg | $ 93.4 | 405,600 | $57b | 29 |
| 2 | Ireland | $ 87.3 | 1,989,400 | $302b | 33.5 |
| 3 | Norway | $ 81.3 | 2,753,000 | $318b | 27.3 |
| 4 | Belgium | $ 69.7 | 4,601,200 | $498b | 29.8 |
| 5 | United States | $ 68.3 | 151,000,000 | $18,037b | 33.6 |

I remember once having an employee who was bent on impressing me with how early he arrived at work (often around 6:30 A.M.) and how late he would stay (usually till about 6:00 P.M.). One day he chose to point out how he worked harder than I and his argument was the hours he was at work. I tried to bite my tongue, but as he kept at it I finally had to say (hopefully in a respectful way), "You know, Tim, you and I must have a different definition of hard work. For me it is not based on hours, it is based on output or productivity." He never brought it up again!

In my work coaching executives, most agree that today's work ethic, in general, seems very different from years past. Hard work and taking personal responsibility for results— good or bad—is not stressed as much. Both qualities are highly valued in organizations, but not emphasized as much at the individual level. These qualities are so simple and basic that we may take them for granted. Television shows used to have a moral to the story—not as much today. Families attended religious services where virtues were taught—not as much today.

Today a word used a lot is "entitlement." I don't want to fall slave to stereotypes here, but let's examine the topic a bit. This is defined as someone who inherently deserves certain privileges or special treatment. This is not a negative word when used in the proper context. If you do a hard day's work, you are entitled to compensation. If you save for retirement, you are entitled to those funds.

You are not, however, entitled to a raise if all you do is just show up for work. I don't mean in the context of consciously showing up and doing excellent work; I mean just being physically present in a designated space and expecting compensation or consideration of a promotion or raise.

In business when we talk about performance management and reinforcement, there is an important difference between a *minimum performance standard* versus *performing beyond the minimum standard*. Essentially, the minimum standard is what is required to remain employed. Performance beyond that is what merits a reward—going beyond the minimum standard.

> Performance beyond what is required merits reward.

The other part of entitlement is the concept of doing the bare minimum, or only doing what you're asked and nothing more. Let's look at a hypothetical example that may not be all that hypothetical. See if this resonates with you.

*You and some friends walk into a restaurant to enjoy a meal. You sit down, and the server comes by about fifteen minutes later and takes the drink order. The server returns twenty minutes later with drinks and says she will be right back to take your order. Fifteen minutes later, after you have eaten all the cracker packets, she takes your order. The drinks are empty, and as she walks away from the table you ask her for a refill—that never happens.*

*The food comes in another twenty-five minutes. It's cold because it was sitting at the window for so long. You've been watching your server talk on her cell phone, laugh with her coworkers at the bar, and talk to her friends who just happened to show up during dinner rush.*

*After starving and then eating a cold meal, she brings you the bill. Every three minutes she returns to see if you have paid it or if she needs to run your credit card. You even ask her again for a drink refill—that never happens. You look at the bill and see the word "tip." What do you do?*

People in the food service industry are probably ready to send me a pointed email about what I'm about to say, but read through it carefully. Wait staff are paid below minimum wage because they rely on you, the customer, to pay the difference. It is really genius on the part of restaurants, because they don't have to pay taxes on tips and they can pay their wait staff next to nothing.

The wait staff must work for their tips. This means that they are providing a service that you the customer must evaluate. The average tip amount is between 15 to 20 percent that is expected. Sometimes if the service is outstanding, you may feel inclined to pay more. But what happens when the service is bad? Are they still entitled to a tip, and if so, how much? A tip is not paid for excellent food, you pay a premium for that; instead, a tip is about paying for a service. So are they entitled?

Let's think about this a step further. What if the restaurant says the tip is "included." Is it really a tip then, or is it a service fee? You have no control over how much that fee is, although it is usually on the high end of 20 percent. Do you pay extra above that for outstanding service? Again, this is an excellent business move on the restaurant's part. They add the fee and pay the wait staff and bartenders their fee, no matter how bad the service was, and they again pass that fee on to you.

### *Great Service and Hard Work Is Noticed*

It's noticeably different when you run across people who demonstrate a strong work ethic—they stand out. Also, they act as an accelerator for getting good work done and more of it. It can be seen as a basic return on investment for what someone is paid.

When the service is outstanding at a business, you remember those people. People who make a good living have figured it out.

# Developing a Work Ethic

As a young boy, I was fascinated to hear stories from my father about his experiences growing up in Salt Lake City and surviving the Great Depression. He painted a picture of very difficult times when up to ten family members were staying in a house that would barely hold four or five. They were all trying to find work to contribute whatever each person could, just to buy food for very meager meals to survive. To help out, my father and his two sisters all worked as children. They would go out each day to find what work they could.

My father, at a very early age, eight or nine, bought eggs from a local farmer. After candling them (holding an egg in front of a candle to see flaws or problems inside the egg shell) for quality, he would sell eggs door to door.

Unless you've been born into independent wealth or inheritance, which eliminates any need for you to earn a living, working to provide for (at minimum) yourself is a pretty basic concept. Or at least it is most common.

My father instilled in me at a very early age the idea that I would have to work to earn a living, and I should learn about work quickly. He also emphasized that it did not matter what I did for a living, but I should do my very best. I've always tried to live up to that expectation.

Hard work is a key to success.

Clearly from the interview data, hard work is thought to be one of the keys to success. One of the people I interviewed is a close friend and has been a mentor to me for many years— Hyler Bracey. Hyler was raised around Gulfport, Mississippi and has led an interesting life. He grew up working at an early age. He had jobs on a tugboat and owned several cotton gins in his 30s. He went on to found a management consulting company that worked with many organizations; he touched a lot of lives in large and small organizations.

Hyler had some great advice for a young person who was starting out in a business:

- Show up early for work.

- Do more than you're asked to do.

- Everything you do, you do to the best of your ability.

- If you finish your work, offer to help others.

These are very powerful differentiators. Following these simple tips eliminates negative entitlement almost completely.

Colin Powell, in his book *It Worked for Me*,[2] lists what great workers look for in high performers or what they see in such people:

1. Someone who consistently demonstrates outstanding performance in different positions.

2. Someone learning and growing intellectually, someone preparing for the next level, not just maxing out in his/her current job; someone who is ambitious but not cutthroat.

3. Someone tested by assignments and challenges generally given to people with more seniority and greater experience, thus indicating early that he/she can probably perform well not only at the higher level but at levels above that one.

4. Someone reaching outside his/her comfort zone to acquire skills and knowledge that are not now essential but are useful at a higher level.

5    Someone who has demonstrated strength of character, moral and physical courage, integrity, and selflessness, and who will carry those virtues to the next level.

6.    Someone who is confident about the next step. His/her ego is under control, and he/she is mentally prepared for the added responsibilities and burdens of higher office. It won't go to his/her head. He/she is balanced.

7.    Someone who enjoys the respect and confidence of his/her contemporaries who may soon become his/her juniors.

Let's talk about doing whatever it takes to produce results that lead to noticeably high performance. There is a wonderful story that has been around for a very long time titled *A Message to Garcia*. I've included the story in Appendix C. It's worth a read. The point of the story is someone who went to extraordinary lengths to produce a result. It really highlights an orientation that is doing whatever it takes to produce a result rather than focusing on why something cannot be done.

The following is a specific approach that will allow you to do the same in your life.

## Personal Responsibility

Early in my career I was exposed to an expression that has stayed with me: *"Performance is measured by results."* It's a simple concept and quite important to remember in most endeavors. When I've forgotten to focus on the desired results, it has often resulted in wasted time and effort. This is a little like what we discussed earlier about purpose. Living life without a clear purpose usually results in wasted time and effort.

The right efforts can lead to great results but do not necessarily guarantee them. You can improve your results by increasing the proper efforts. It is easy to say, "Well, I tried." There are no performance awards given for trying; they are given for results. If you are not achieving results, look at why and make the necessary adjustments. Figure out where you need to inject more effort and energy, and at the same time assess where you are wasting your time.

This is important because many people say they are "busy." Yes, being busy takes effort. Yes, being busy shows you are making an effort. But being busy does *not* create results. This quote is great way to remember:

> Activity is not productivity without a clearly defined desired result.

It is amazing how much energy some people put into looking and appearing busy rather than focusing on results. Remember the story of my "long hours" employee! I had to tell him that I was not necessarily impressed with long hours but rather results. Some who put in long hours do so because they are less efficient.

Inherent in following this line of logic is being clear about what the desired results are and, second, being committed to producing those results. Nike's famous slogan is "Just do it," and in every setting I've seen the emphasis on and rewards for getting the right things done. In the work setting, those who produce results achieve higher levels of success.

Let's look at Question 2 in my survey again:

**Question 2**: What two or three qualities or personality traits have most contributed to your own success in business and in life?

- Hard work

- Persistence

- Strong work ethic

- Willingness to do whatever necessary

Having a hard-work ethic is prevalent as a differentiator.

# Barriers to High Performance

As I have coached many people, I occasionally witness the opposite behavior—not producing results. As always, I try to find the root cause, because one of my fundamental beliefs is that most people have good intentions; they want to do the right thing. Invariably when I see others who repeatedly fail to produce desired results, it's due to a systemic issue—it is a fundamental orientation that leads to some unproductive behaviors.

I offer the following "best practice" to establish a proper foundation for producing the desired results repeatedly and eliminating behaviors that typically get in the way. Beyond being successful in life, if you can work on this concept it will help you get more of what you really want in life. Let's take a look.

# 100 Percent Responsibility

You may have noticed that when something goes wrong there is seldom a rush of individuals to accept responsibility for the problem. You have probably heard of CYA (Cover Your A@@). In organizations, politics, and even families, much effort is spent blaming someone or justifying why a problem occurred. Usually the effort goes into avoiding being identified as the culprit.

The legal profession has developed assigning blame as an art form, and unfortunately our litigious society rewards the opposite of individuals holding themselves accountable for their own behavior.

I present to you a concept called 100 percent responsibility.

I can already hear, "But…." But no one can be 100 percent responsible for everything in life. This may be true, but everyone *can choose* to be 100 percent responsible for producing desired results.

This concept, while very simple, is frequently difficult for some to adopt. The idea is reasonably novel and therefore some resist it. Dismissing this concept too quickly will work to your disadvantage, so I encourage you to maintain an open mind and consider the possibilities as you read. Your only real risk is the time invested to read and the effort in making the concept work for you. The beauty of this concept is that it will work whether you believe it will or not. The act of trying produces the result. So give it a shot—the downside is slim, if any.

The first time I was presented with this concept I was both intrigued and resistant. I was also a little disappointed as I considered my own past attempts at getting off the hook. I know my friends and relatives would be happy to point out specific examples.

I knew things had to change, so I shifted my thinking and therefore my actions. I decided that I am 100 percent responsible for what happens in my life and everyone else is 0 percent responsible. There is no 50-50 or even 100-100. It was me 100 percent! There is no one else to blame—period, end of discussion. Whatever happens, I did it. If the result was achieved, I did it; if not, I did it.

I was resistant to this concept the first time I heard about it; even the second and third time I was really skeptical. Clearly there are situations in my world over which I have no control. To think that I was solely responsible for the results in my life was too big a leap for me to make. In fact, it took me several times sitting through the presentation and gracious coaching from my mentors to finally realize what the value could be. It really sank in when I realized that if I applied the principle, it worked whether I believed it would or not.

Acting as if I'm 100 percent responsible forces me to move forward. I don't wait for or rely on anyone else to produce the result for me. A key point here is that *I still can ask for help* because it is one of the options I exercise to produce the result. Ultimately, however, *I alone am responsible for producing the result.*

The reason that the ratio must be 100 percent to 0 percent is that as long as the zero spot is occupied by any value, I can blame or justify the non-result. That is why the best approach to any two-party relationship is where both parties assume the 100 percent to 0 percent position. Potentially neither party will blame or justify if the relationship result is not produced. Consider how your relationship at home, work, etc. would be if no one blamed or justified when something fell short of the desired result. Most importantly, consider how the world would be if more people invested energy in producing the desired result rather than blaming or justifying when something went wrong.

Many are familiar with the legal case against a large fast food chain when an individual purchased and then spilled hot coffee on herself. Like me, perhaps you wondered where the personal responsibility was in that example. Entitlement is the enemy of personal responsibility. The woman was entitled to compensation for nothing more than spilling coffee on herself.

The motive for such behavior might be to avoid being the culprit. However, this behavior has a serious downside— namely, it is ineffective in creating a result you really want.

Bottom line: blaming and justifying *limits* options and 100 percent to 0 percent responsibility *expands* options. Obviously, this concept is not a panacea and will not correct all the problems of the world. It will, however, increase your own personal power and, in the process, allow you to get more of what you truly want in life.

> Excuses are not desired results.

For anyone who ascribes to the CYA mentality, excuses are the stock in trade. Many would think the following equation is accurate:

Desired Results = No Desired Results + Excuse

"The report wasn't completed because my computer crashed," or "I lost my Internet connection," or "Your car isn't ready because we had big rush of customers and fell behind."

In both cases it appears that the speaker by virtue of providing the excuse is off the hook and the excuse makes up for the fact that the result was not produced. For the supervisor or customer, you know that the existence of the excuse has not replaced the desired result. Accepting excuses reinforces wrong behaviors, and the result is more ingenious excuses and few desired results.

> Accepting excuses reinforces wrong behaviors.

To illustrate how ridiculous this formula is, consider the following example. My desired result is a salary increase. I get no increase because there was a sales downturn. Therefore:

Salary Increase = No Salary Increase + Sales Downturn

There is no way that equation will ever be equal. You can't pay bills with excuses. "No result" with an excuse will never produce the result. There is another word people don't like to hear, but I am going to write it—*accountability*. You are accountable 100 percent for the choices you make. You are accountable 100 percent for the results you produce or don't produce.

Consider this statement: "I couldn't get the report done because I was too sick, my kids were sick, and eventually the dog was sick."

Who is responsible for the report being completed? Well…you are! Who is accountable for the report not getting completed? Again, you. So will an excuse relieve you of responsibility or accountability? No, not unless your boss decides to give the responsibility to someone else—and fire you.

# Blaming and Justifying

Two of the most common forms of excuse are blaming and *justifying*. Each of us may have been on either end from time to time. Let's look at these individually.

### *Blaming*

Consider whether you've heard or have said something similar to the following:

- "That's not my fault. Mary was supposed to do that."

- "That's not my job. Robert's in charge of that."

- "The problem is, Fred didn't follow through."

- "It's hung up in accounts payable."

Blaming shifts the focus away from the person responsible, or accountable, to someone else. In the short run it may allow us to save face, but it is a disabling behavior. When considering the impact of blaming, you are making the other person responsible—and you put that person in control of the situation. To produce the desired result, *the other person* has to take action.

As a trainer, sometimes sessions don't go as I planned. Before learning the seriousness of blaming, my reaction was to blame the audience for not participating or not being attentive enough. After learning what blaming actually does, when I was confronted with a tough group or session I adjusted my behavior to examine what I could do to improve the result I was producing.

The act of creating options for improvement always puts me in control, and instead of *disabling* myself I *enable* myself. I realized that expecting the group to change to meet my expectations was rarely going to produce the result I wanted. I was giving away my power to improve the outcome. That is why blaming is a disabling behavior. It prevents us from learning and changing in response to undesirable situations and is a barrier to producing more of the results we want.

As with any concept, we have to inject a dose of reality. The truth is, we often are faced with obstacles that are just the nature of life. The important thing is to acknowledge a missed result or broken agreement first and then convey how to correct it. Some examples of how to do this would be: "I'm sorry the report isn't ready. I'm working on it right now and will bring it to you before noon tomorrow." And, "I'm calling because your car will not be ready at the time we agreed on. I will deliver your car to your work or home before 4 o'clock today after ensuring the problem is completely fixed. I'm very sorry for the delay." And, "I'm contacting you the day before the report is due because I have the flu and want you to know that John is finishing the report for me. He has all the data I compiled and will submit it to you on time. Thank you for understanding." Notice that these responses incorporate some of the guidance from "Management by Agreement" reviewed on page 98.

### Justifying

Another common form of excuse is *justification,* and you can probably think of situations where someone justified not producing a result you wanted or expected. Consider my example of being sick and not completing a report on time. There is nothing a person can do about being sick. It happens, but what really differentiates a person is the commitment to seeing a project or promise through no matter what. It is easy to justify; it takes a solid work ethic to find a way to make it right.

Here are some common justifications:

- "Let me explain why I did it that way."

- "There was nothing anyone could do."

- "That happened because…"

Justifying is a means to explain a non-result or blame a situation for not producing the desired result, and again it shifts the focus of control away from us.

The obvious question is—why do folks do so much blaming and justifying? While motivations are different, I can offer insights from my experience. When I blame or justify, it allows me to be right. If I am right, it is often at the expense of someone else. Being right always seems more appealing than being wrong because I can save face. Unfortunately, being right is a poor substitute for not producing the desired result, especially because I am choosing to be less effective than I could be. Blaming and justifying put us at the mercy of other people and events and there is no improvement.

It is also used as a way to deflect the limelight. No one likes being in the hot seat and explaining why something did not happen or why the results were not as expected.

So, consider how great the world would be without blaming or justifying non-results. Easier said than done, right?

When working to eliminate an unacceptable behavior, it is helpful to replace it with a new, better behavior. This is exactly what I propose to you. To be truly *100 percent responsible for producing the desired results,* it is critical to generate options to produce the desired result.

Producing options is the key behavior to replace blaming and justifying. If you have not produced the desired result, it's helpful to keep exploring options. Sometimes in a sticky situation it may take a while and lots of options to consider. The key is, if you are focused on generating options to produce a desired result, it is virtually impossible to blame or justify.

For example, if you accept a project that is slightly outside your realm of expertise but you're sure you can accomplish the task, think about who can provide knowledge, research a variety of resources you can tap into to fill the gaps, and reach out to colleagues for a team effort. Of course, giving credit to these collaborators is the right thing to do—and will distinguish you as a person of moral character.

Again, this concept works whether you believe it will or not.

## Three Principles

The following are three principles that are worthy of committing to memory:

1. Routinely focus on taking responsibility for your actions and inactions.

2. Be a person who can be held accountable, who is trustworthy.

3.   Consider any and all options to produce the results you committed to producing.

# Now What?

1.   At work, put in place these four simple principles from my friend Hyler:

     ▪   Show up early for work.

     ▪   Do more than you're asked to do.

     ▪   Do everything to the best of your ability.

     ▪   If you finish your work, offer to help others.

2.   Be willing to monitor yourself for a week or two. On Friday, look back and evaluate how well you did. Can you cite specific examples of each of the four principles?

3.   Post the list from Colin Powell in a place close to your work area as a reminder.

4.   Consider for several weeks how well you are living the principles of *100 percent responsibility:*

     ▪   Notice in particular whether you *blame* or *justify* when a desired result is not produced.

     ▪   How effective are you in continuing to generate options to produce desired results?

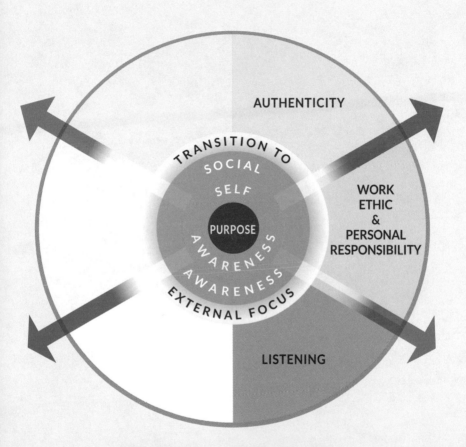

# DIFFERENTIATOR 3—
# LISTENING

# CHAPTER 7

# LISTENING FOR RESULTS AND CONNECTIONS

*"A man hears what he wants to hear
and he disregards the rest."*
—SIMON AND GARFUNKEL, "THE BOXER"

LISTENING—Concentrate intently on the words of others in such a way you could understand and repeat accurately what is said.

THE NEXT TWO CHAPTERS GO TOGETHER—ONE IS ABOUT listening and the other is about verbal communication. Steven Covey, in his book *The 7 Habits of Highly Effective People,* writes, "Seek first to understand, then to be understood."[1]

This is why I chose to start with listening in order to understand others before we spend time talking about how to be understood. As the old saying goes, "We have two ears and one mouth so that we can listen twice as much as we speak."

# Getting Inside

To truly "seek to understand" someone, you have to slip into that person's frame of reference. This includes understanding the person's values, experience, knowledge, and emotion. You have to understand the elements of the other person, how the person ticks. You must try to climb into the person's head and experience the world as he or she does.

The best way to get into someone else's frame of reference is to listen.

There is a difference between *hearing* someone speak and *listening* to someone speak. Determining the difference is often a challenge in marriages. For example, I've been part of the following scenario. A husband may nod his head and say affirming words while his wife is talking, but when she stops talking and he looks at her face, her expression says, "I just asked you a question and I am waiting for an answer." The husband hits rewind on his internal tape to try to remember what his wife just said twenty seconds prior. No good. He was hearing her talk, but he had not truly listened and absorbed what she said. So the only logical thing for him to say is something like, "Could you say that again?" Of course, at this point he's doomed.

Have you ever sat through a two-hour meeting, and then the boss turns to the person next to you and asks the dreaded question, "So what do you think?"

If the guy was passively listening, sweat will begin to glisten on his brow, and he might stutter something like, "Well (boss)…I, uh…don't know. I'll have to think about that. I'll get back to you later."

What everyone else in the room hears him say: "I was thinking about lunch and whether I should clean my garage this weekend. I have no idea what you were saying, because it really is not that important to me. So instead of admitting I was tuning you out, I'm going to make up a lame response to woefully cover my tracks."

Abbott and Costello were a comedy team who performed in a number of shows and movies together. One of their most famous bits was "Who's on first?" The following is a short excerpt of a very funny routine.

> Costello: That's what I want to find out. I want you to tell me the names of the fellows on the St. Louis team.
>
> Abbott: I'm telling you. Who's on first, What's on second, I Don't Know is on third.
>
> Costello: You know the fellows' names?
>
> Abbott: Yes.
>
> Costello: Well, then who's playing first?
>
> Abbott: Yes.
>
> Costello: I mean the fellow's name on first base.
>
> Abbott: Who.
>
> Costello: The fellow playin' first base.
>
> Abbott: Who.
>
> Costello: The guy on first base.
>
> Abbott: Who is on first.
>
> Costello: Well, what are you askin' me for?
>
> Abbott: I'm not asking you, I'm telling you. Who is on first.

Costello: I'm asking you, who's on first?

Abbott: That's the man's name.

Costello: That's who's name?

Abbott: Yes.

You can watch the entire skit on YouTube. It's well worth the time.

When performed, it matched great writing with well-practiced timing and resulted in Lou Costello being completely exasperated at the end of the bit. Beyond being hilarious, it's a good example of many personal interactions today. Think about interactions you have had in the recent past with any number of people or even some you've witnessed. I bet you can think of times when the conversation clearly felt or looked out of sync. Two people were talking, some information might have been exchanged, but they were not really communicating— not really connecting. Basic, focused connection is critical to successful, respectful relationships. It is also quite critical to accomplishing tasks with other individuals—it's crucial for effective collaboration.

The first survey question I asked was: *Think of one or two very successful (in business and life) individuals you've witnessed/admired in your career. What two or three questions or personality traits in those successful individuals do you believe most contributed to their success?*

A common answer: They are great listeners. But what does that mean? What are the essential parts of being a great listener?

For years, I have used a simple definition for effective communication: *When a sender sends information to an intended receiver, and the intended receiver hears and understands the information in the way the sender intended.*

This definition is elegant in its simplicity. However, it is somewhat fragile when you consider all the elements and realize that if even one of the elements is missing, effective communication will not occur. You can see that both people are responsible for the outcome.

Paying attention and being able to focus are pertinent skills to have in any career, but they are critical in my line of work. I've learned a lot by paying attention to speakers, which is imperative when advising corporate leaders on an improved course of action. I must be able to provide context for advice and counsel. My credibility is enhanced by providing details. It's a skill anyone can learn. Paying attention to details makes me look a lot smarter than I probably am.

Learning to pay attention starts with a profoundly simple behavior—*listening!* It's a simple idea in short supply in many settings. I don't mean pretending to listen. I mean genuinely listening. And I mean *listening for full meaning* of the speaker's message.

> There is a difference between hearing someone speak and listening to someone speak.

You have probably been in conversations where a lot of people are talking, and you wonder if a message or information is actually being heard and received. Bar conversations are often great examples of this type of superficial conversation. I teach

131

the art of listening in some of my workshops, and to improve listening it's helpful to consider what gets in the way of listening. For example, I grew up in a family that ate dinner together almost every night, and Mom and Dad were great about encouraging dinner table discussions about a variety of topics. My parents and older sisters were intelligent people, and as the "baby" of the family I envied their exchanges and always wanted to participate (whether I really understood the topic or not).

It was hard to get a word in, so I developed a behavior of picking out certain bits of the conversation and then thought about what to say in response. I got pretty good at formulating a response while the other person was talking. The problem, though, was that I wasn't really listening to the whole message, so I missed a lot of important information. That habit carried over into my adult life and started to reflect poorly on me and affected my performance. I found myself in the very uncomfortable position of feeling uninformed and often not offering very intelligent responses. Also, my responses were often emotional and reactive rather than thoughtful and deliberate.

In my workshops, I often ask, "Is listening an observable behavior?" Easily more than 95 percent of the people answer, "Yes."

Then I ask, "What does listening look like?"

Common answers are: "People have wide, open eyes and maintain eye contact. They lean forward, and nod their heads."

And I then ask, "What is the acid test that real listening actually occurred?"

Very few people easily answered this, yet the answer is fairly simple: *You know people have listened to you if they can demonstrate they heard.*

This is so important because in the process of a dialog or conversation, *listening is not truly an observable behavior.* Considering the common listening behavior answers I receive (wide open eyes, maintain eye contact, lean forward, and nodding heads), can you demonstrate those behaviors without actually listening? Of course you can, and many often do.

Active listening accelerates communication and understanding. By doing it well you can build trust and demonstrate respect for others. Most people love the sound of their own voice; a basic need developed at an early age for all humans is to be heard. We create connection by addressing that need.

To significantly improve your listening, let's consider other typical barriers to effective listening I've encountered in my work with organizations.

### Ego

At one point in my life, I helped design and deliver sales training for my company. Listening was one of the key sales skill sets we emphasized, and we looked at why salespeople sometimes don't listen. Often we found it was because they were so focused on what they wanted to say—almost without thinking of the purpose or impact. They were poised to be reactive to just a portion of what the client was saying rather than being submerged in the entirety of the speaker's conversation. A helpful mnemonic we used was, *"Be interested rather than interesting!"*

### Interrupting

Most children are taught that it's rude to interrupt when others are speaking. It goes beyond being rude, however;

interrupting means that the interrupter is not listening for the full message and meaning.

Another variation of interruptions is *finishing sentences for the other person.* Many do this out of impatience, thinking, *Just get to the point!* The issue, of course, is again beyond being rude or disrespectful; it means we aren't *listening for full meaning.* If your focus is on how to finish the sentence, you aren't concentrating on what is being said. The interesting thing is, when I stop myself from finishing the sentence, more than 50 percent of the time the person doesn't finish the thought the way I would have.

### *Emotion*

Another barrier to effective listening is the emotional atmosphere of the conversation. When we are emotionally hooked into a conversation, we tend to focus more on reacting and less on truly listening. Emotion causes us to focus inwardly on ourselves rather than focusing outwardly on the other person. It can also cause our responses to be reactive and irrational rather than thoughtful and calm.

Differences between responsive and reactive:

- Responsive: greater thought, less speed

- Reactive: greater speed, less thought

## There's no such thing as multitasking

*Multitasking* is a commonly used word. But I submit that there is no such thing as multitasking. Your brain can only process one thing at a time.

For example, have you ever stubbed your toe, and while you are hopping around you whack your elbow? All of a sudden, you're holding your arm and lamenting the pain there. What happened to the injured toe? The pain is still there, but you aren't aware of it because your focus is on the pain in your arm.

What we think of as multitasking is really the ability to switch from one task to another at high rates of speed. This is one of the reasons people are told not to text and drive—because they cannot fully engage in driving when their attention is looking at a phone screen. They may hear a horn blowing or see a red light, but drivers cannot focus at the same time on a text and a car that stopped suddenly in front of them. The brain shifts back and forth—often just in time to rear-end the car in front of them.

How does this translate to conversations? Let's look at what might happen if you text during a meeting. The type in bold is someone speaking and the italicized text is someone typing.

**Today, we are going to review last quarter's numbers. First we...**

> *Where do u want 2 go 2 dinner tonight?*
> *How about the new Mexican restaurant?*

**Our projections for the next month is to decrease spending in each department...**

> *I don't like Mexican, how 'bout Italian?*
> *I love Italian. Pizza or pasta?*
> *Pasta.*

**Thank you for your attention and understanding. I know this will be hard for each of you, but I'm sure you understand the cuts we have to make. I have confidence that you can explain to your teams why this is necessary. So if there are no further questions, have a great rest of your day.**

What just happened? The person who was present at the meeting heard the words but wasn't focused on what was being said. He could hear what was being said, but at the end of the meeting he knew he missed something important. Well, at least he knows he's having pasta for dinner, which could be the last time he eats out if he loses his job.

## Listen to the Music Behind the Words

As I mentioned previously, it is important to understand people's frame of reference—their mindset or worldview. This is how they see and react to the world around them. Listening to their words gives you insight to their personal vision, but to dig deeper you must listen to the "music behind the words." This includes discovering *why* they believe the things they do. What makes them happy and sad? What shaped and shapes their world? What do they think is their purpose?

By being a great listener, you make a conscious connection with people—one they will not soon forget. You will become important to them—and this is why listening is a key differentiator. Anyone can share their ideas and thoughts. Just listen to conversations at a coffee shop or at the office—or even read it on Facebook. Everyone has opinions, but rare are those individuals who can listen, reflect, and make a conscious connection with someone else.

## Reflective Listening

Start listening to others with the express intent of being able to repeat back to the individual precisely what they said. This is reflective listening. Sometimes it is exactly what they said word for word, or you repeat the meaning as you decoded it to be.

The following is an example of a conversation where one person is listening reflectively:

> **Bob:** *"The project is tanking, and people are counting on us. I don't think we're going to get it done on time...and even if we do, it won't meet the boss's expectations."*
>
> **Susan:** *"So you think this project won't meet the boss's standards and we aren't going to meet our deadline?"*
>
> **Bob:** *"Yes, but I'm also worried that we're going to let the team down."*
>
> **Susan:** *"So it's important we do a great job because others are watching and are expecting great things from us?"*
>
> **Bob:** *"Exactly!"*

Some key points:

- This technique is nothing new—it's often called "parroting" or "doing a listening check." It's been around a while because it's effective—it works.

- When used correctly, the person actually repeats what has been said—that way both people are certain of what was said and the intent is clear.

- This technique is seldom practiced today—and there are many miscommunications.

- It requires concentration and focus to do it well. You must be actively listening—focused only on what the other person is saying, not multitasking.

- When you practice this technique, you will significantly improve your listening skill to the point where you don't actually have to repeat what's been said, it becomes a habit.

- Is this tactic appropriate for every conversation? Certainly in any you deem important, the answer is yes. Maybe not in casual or social conversations, although it's a great way to remember a person's name.

It's harder to *really* pay attention today due to the many possible distractions, especially all of our technology gadgets. The other reason paying attention or focus is such an important behavior or skill, is that in human interaction it is a sign of basic respect.

## Social Awareness

How can you be aware of what is going on around you if you don't listen? Start now to listen to what is being said around you. If you are talking or distracted, you are probably missing information that could help you at work, socially, relationally, etc.

Being a "fly on the wall" has a distinct advantage. You can pick up information that keeps you abreast of what is happening around you at work, in your community, state, and nation. Often it is the talk before or after a meeting that has the best information, and people often let their guard down enough to speak the "truth."

Good listeners always know what is going on and can anticipate what will happen next. Good listeners appear to not only care more, but they appear to be smarter too. This is because they take time to express themselves before they speak. We will be covering this in more depth in the next chapter.

## Now What?

Work on the skills and techniques discussed in this chapter and consciously notice the impact of each when interacting with others.

1.  Consciously make an agreement to periodically listen reflectively. I often use the following language: "I want to be sure I fully heard and understood you. I heard you say _____ _____." I will often wrap up by saying, "Did I get it right?"

2.  Pay particular attention to when you missed something important that was said. In time, you will get very good at this if you focus on it. My experience is that your relationships will be enhanced.

> "Listening is such a simple act. It requires us to be present, and that takes practice, but we don't have to do anything else. We don't have to advise, or coach, or sound wise. We just have to be willing to sit there and listen."
> —Margaret Wheatley, *Finding Our Way*

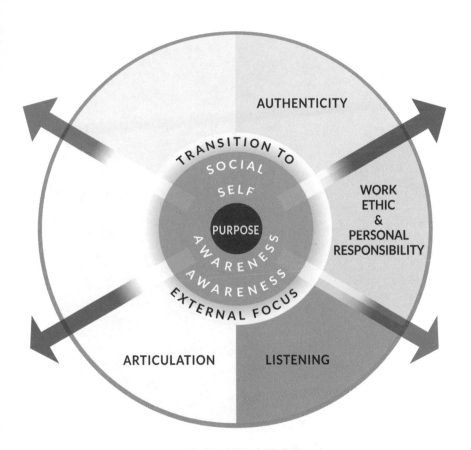

AUTHENTICITY

WORK ETHIC & PERSONAL RESPONSIBILITY

TRANSITION TO

SOCIAL

SELF

PURPOSE

AWARENESS

AWARENESS

EXTERNAL FOCUS

ARTICULATION

LISTENING

# DIFFERENTIATOR 4—
# ARTICULATION

# CHAPTER 8

# ARTICULATION FOR IMPACT

*"It is better to remain silent and thought a
fool than to speak and remove all doubt."*
—MAURICE SWITZER

---

ARTICULATION—Provide information in a clear,
concise way which produces the desired impact.

---

CITED PREVIOUSLY, MY EFFECTIVE COMMUNICATION DEFINItion is when a sender sends information to an intended receiver, and the intended receiver hears and understands the information in the way the sender intended.

Clear, concise, direct communications accelerate your ability to get your thoughts put into action. I believe it is fundamental to our human condition that we want to be heard. This is also why the previous differentiator—listening—is so critical and precedes this one. Being heard and understood is a basic need of most people, reinforced as we grow up by conversing with others, which is the most simple and obvious of human interactions.

Performance and results in businesses, organizations, and every group effort are dependent on effective flow of information. In working with many teams over the years, communication is often cited as a common challenge.

Growing up, I was fairly impatient and probably spent more time talking when I should have been listening. I can think of times when I said things I regretted, often because I wanted to hear the sound of my own voice. That is often true for many who operate with low self-awareness. Often what I had to say wasn't really all that important. I was fortunate to have great role models from whom I learned throughout the years.

After how we look, how we communicate is the next most noticeable when we meet someone for the first time. Being articulate will cause the person to remember you—in a good way.

## Vocabulary

I learned about proper grammar and spelling from my sister who was an elementary school teacher. So what I didn't learn or had forgotten from elementary through high school, she was more than ready to help. I received a lot of unsolicited feedback when my communication and spelling were subpar (which was often, apparently!). She set a good example in her communication as did my dad and others in business for whom I had a lot of respect. Because I respected them, I wanted to emulate them. Over the years I noticed patterns in people I admired.

One of the key tools is a well-developed vocabulary. Having options for conveying ideas to various audiences is a huge plus. Communicating effectively to different audiences demonstrates great social awareness. Having a command of language helps articulate our ideas, thoughts, and emotions more clearly.

You probably know the book *Green Eggs and Ham,* written by Dr. Seuss (a pen-name of Theodor Seuss Geisel). What you may not know about this book is that it only contains fifty different words. When Geisel had finished writing *The Cat in the Hat,* which contained 225 different words, Geisel's publisher, Bennett Cerf, bet Geisel $50 that he could not create an entire book using only fifty words.[1]

The point is, if you can write a book or read one with only fifty words, why would you need a larger vocabulary?

The average adult has an active vocabulary of about 20,000 words and a passive vocabulary of about 40,000 words according to Susie Dent, a lexicographer and expert in dictionaries.

An active vocabulary is one you use to write with and use in everyday conversation; a passive vocabulary is comprised of words you can read and understand but do not necessarily use. Of course, expanding your active vocabulary makes you appear smarter and also allows you to be clearer in what you are expressing. I'm not saying you should be a walking dictionary, but having a well-developed vocabulary is a definite differentiator.

From the *Reading Teacher's Book of Lists,* of the 20,000 active words:

- The first 25 words are used in 33 percent of everyday writing.

- The first 100 words appear in 50 percent of adult and student writing.

- The first 1,000 words are used in 89 percent of everyday writing.

- A vocabulary of just 3,000 words provides coverage for around 95 percent of common texts (such as news items, blogs, etc.).[2]

## Study Data

**Question 4**: When considering one of your most challenging times or a time when you made a mistake and had to deal with it in the best way, what action or characteristic or thought helped you get through the adversity?

There were a number of responses to this question that indicated good communication skills were essential in these types of situations. This makes sense, as any tough situation is never solved emotionally or in a vacuum. Problems and issues are talked out, and clear solutions and strategies are then possible.

But what does this type of clear communication look like? What does it include? I refer you to the definition of communication again: *When a sender sends information to an intended receiver, and the intended receiver hears and understands the information in the way the sender intended.*

Let's look at what is known as the constructionist model of communication.

According to this model, there is a pattern of communication that exists.

## THE CONSTRUCTIONIST MODEL OF COMMUNICATION

| | |
|---|---|
| **Noise:** | Interference with effective transmission and reception of a message. |
| **Sender:** | The initiator and encoder of a message. |
| **Receiver:** | The one who receives the message (the listener) and the decoder of a message. |
| **Decode:** | The receiver translates the sender's spoken idea/message into something the receiver understands by using their knowledge of language from personal experience. |
| **Encode:** | Sender puts the idea into spoken language while putting their own meaning into the word/message. |
| **Channel:** | The medium through which the message travels such as through oral communication (radio, television, phone, in person) or written communication (letters, email, text messages) |
| **Feedback:** | The receiver's verbal and nonverbal responses to a message such as a nod for understanding (nonverbal), a raised eyebrow for being confused (nonverbal), or asking a question to clarify the message (verbal). |
| **Message:** | The verbal and nonverbal components of language that are sent to the receiver by the sender, which convey an idea. |

It seems like there is a lot going on in this model, but if you think of any communication it really can be broken down this way. If there is a problem with any one of these parts, there will be an issue, so it is a good guide to figure out where a breakdown may be occurring.

Let's examine the model even more closely:

- **Noise:** Is the person speaking loudly or clearly enough for others to hear? Have you ever been in a meeting or conference where you can't hear the person speaking? This can be a serious problem. Noise can be the written word as well. Imagine using the wrong language in your communication. This is a simple issue to recognize and fix, but it needs to be done quickly to ensure the message is being clearly transmitted.

- **Sender**: Who is speaking? Whose turn is it to speak? Have you been in a situation where many people are talking at once? No one can be sure to whom they should be listening. Develop a way to acknowledge who has the floor to speak.

- **Receiver**: Are people paying attention? Or are they on their smartphone checking email? One sure-fire way to know if the receiver is paying attention is to have clear eye contact. Have everyone put their phones in a basket before a meeting. Some people are almost addicted to their link to cyberspace, so eliminating that distraction will assure you of their attention.

- **Decode:** As the sender, you need to be sure that the people are decoding the message you are sending. Do they seem to understand? Do they seem distracted? You need to be sure you have their undivided attention as well as ask them periodically if they understand and have any questions. This is about being "present." As the receiver, you must be attentive and ask questions for clarification. See the last chapter about active listening.

- **Encode**: This is one of the most difficult parts of communication. Are you using your language skills to clearly communicate what you are saying or writing? It might take rephrasing and trying different ways to explain something. Illustrations, stories, and analogies are great ways to explain and encode your message. Be creative and be prepared to try different ways to encode. As a sender, you must understand that different people decode ideas in different ways. Sometimes it is based on their learning style or their personality style. You must learn how to encode for individuals as well as large audiences.

- **Channel**: We live in a wonderful age in which we can change mediums for communication, many of which are instantaneous through electronic devices. It is hard to write a complete thought in 140 characters, so if you want to communicate something clearly you should pay attention to the medium you are using. Does it make more sense to send an email than use instant chat? Or does it make more sense to pick up the phone? Or better yet, should you set up a meeting to talk to someone face to face?

■ **Feedback**: This is essential for both the sender and the receiver. The sender knows that the receiver was listening and, more importantly, that the message was understood or needed clarification. It is the receiver's responsibility to ask questions, informing the sender that the message is understood or not. Unless, of course, they are professional mind readers.

■ **Message**: In professional settings, lose the emojis and the text talk, which is one step away from pictographs on cave walls. Use real words and proper spelling and grammar. Having command of written and oral language is a huge differentiator and conveys the message that you care about your message and the person receiving it.

## Different Channels

Words are not the only way we communicate. There is also tone of voice and body language that provide a significant amount of context and subtext to the words you are speaking. The pitch, power, and pace of your speech can affect the meaning of the words. You know when someone is emotional or upset by their pitch and volume. These determinants are not possible when a person is sending an email, text, or letter. These mediums require adjectives and adverbs to elicit emotional sub-text, so it is very important to use them.

The pace, or speed, at which we speak is more important than you may think. The average person speaks about 110 to 130 words per minute, but professional speakers speak closer to 150 to 160 words per minute, and auctioneers are in the 250-wpm range.

When you can slow down your pace and take pauses, you rewrite the music of the spoken word. Pauses and silence allow you to think and process, as they also do for the receiver. Have you ever been in a conversation with someone who speaks at the pace of a racecar on a super-highway? Trying to carry on a conversation with this type of communicator is like driving a compact car in the merge lane trying to figure out a way to get in the flow of fast-moving traffic. You wait politely for an opening to speak—that never happens. Many times you never get a word in. If the pace is slowed with pauses, it allows others to talk and express their ideas and give you feedback.

Sometimes, being in a person's presence is essential. Even video chats lack the benefit of time one on one. In person, you can read people's body language. You can feel if they are present and really locked in to what you're talking about. You are present.

Generally speaking, we can evaluate communication mediums from most effective to least effective according to the following:

1.  Face to face, common language

2.  Technological face to face, common language—
    Skype, video conference, etc.

3. Face to face, uncommon language

4. Audio, common language

5 Written, common language—memo/letter, email, etc.

6. Text—has its own language for many

7. Written uncommon language

8. Smoke signals

Today we rely heavily on texting and emails as primary channels of communication, but so much can be lost in translation. If you are feeling frustrated over a conversation, set up a meeting with the person *in person.* You cannot read emotions from a smiley face. They cannot convey what a genuine smile can convey.

If you work from home or have many people working off site, schedule time to meet with people to mingle and exchange ideas. That is where real innovations happen, not in a text.

*ATM having tough time. Need advice @TEOTD. Need AFPOE and QSO. CM*

NP. CWYL.

*At the moment I'm having a tough time with the project. I need your advice at the end of the day. I need a fresh pair of eyes and an in-depth conversation. Call me.*

No problem. Chat with you later.

What does this exchange really convey? You know the person is having a tough time, but a tough time with what? How are they feeling about it? What info do they need? Is there anything this person needs? What needs to get moving and when?

These sorts of texts are sent every day, prompting guessing games between senders and receivers. This is the best reply to that text:

> *Can I call you to clarify? Or can we meet in your office at 5 today?*

Seems obvious, right? But how many times do people become frustrated and spend hours typing responses and shooting emails back and forth when a five-minute chat would clarify everything?

## Foundation Framework for Conscious Success

### *Purpose*

What is the purpose of your message? What do you hope it will achieve? Providing facts, queries, responses, greetings, invitations, etc. Regarding email messages, there is nothing worse than sending (or receiving) a revenge email. When you are upset and want to dump all of your thoughts and emotions—do not write an email. If you have to write your feelings, use pencil and paper—and then a shredder. Never underestimate the power of words. They can cut or they can elevate—and they can haunt if used harshly.

Are your messages consistent with your purpose? Are the words and ideas you include consistent with your personal brand? You do not want your differentiation motto to be, "Do as I say, not as I do." Or worse, "Do as I do, not as I say." This causes confusing messages that can hurt your credibility or trustworthiness. Be consistent. Remember, the Internet is forever. Whatever you put out there is likely to be out there for as long as the Internet exists. You can bury it, but you can never really delete it.

Be sure you pay attention to what you say on social media. You are what you tweet! Employers vet people through social media. What are you posting? Is it consistent with the company brand? News travels fast, and social media travels at the speed of light. There is no real privacy in emails, Facebook, LinkedIn, or any other online social media platform. You can always hit the delete key before you post something, but once it's out there, it's out there. You are judged by what and how you write.

### *Self-Awareness*

Ask yourself, *What is my emotional state right now and how might it influence what I'm about to say or write?*

You not only have to be aware of the words you use but the emotions and state of mind behind them. Even though written language does not convey emotional states as do verbal and visual communication, it still has an emotional state that can bleed through. Take time to consider your frame of mind and check your gut—if you're reacting out of anger or hurt or without having all the facts, *hold off sending that text, email, fax, or letter.* It can save so much grief and misunderstanding.

If there is not a time element to a communication, type it and then walk away from it for a bit. Come back and read it with fresh eyes. Remember, once you send it, it's gone. Also, take time to edit for spelling and typos; your work reflects on your work ethic.

### *Social Awareness*

What is my intent in saying or writing this? What impact do I want to make on the recipient(s)?

Use the best, most articulate words for maximum impact. People are being bombarded with communications from every angle every day—and night. From texting and instant messaging to Facebook and Twitter, not to forget billboards, television, radio, YouTube, and the millions of websites yearning to grab your attention. Society is overflowing with written and spoken words. Choose carefully how you present yourself to the world through your words and speech.

Tip: The following does not create positive impact when writing professionally:

- **Bolding everything**

- Underlining everything

- *Italicizing everything*

- Highlighting everything.

- Using tons of exclamation points!!!!!!

Words have impact. Use them wisely and correctly.

# Now What?

1. Improve your vocabulary. Learn a new word every day. There are calendars that can help you. Use the word in the sentence at least three times, and you will own the word. Do crossword puzzles. This is an excellent way to build vocabulary. When you are reading, have a dictionary

nearby. Don't just gloss over words you don't know; look them up.

2. Video record yourself with both prepared remarks and extemporaneous talk. How effective did it look to you? What did you like/dislike/want to change?

"Wise men speak because they have something to say; fools because they have to say something."

—A Proverb

# DIFFERENTIATOR 5— HUMOR

# CHAPTER 9

# HUMOR

*"Outside of a dog, a book is man's best friend.*
*Inside of a dog, it's too dark to read."*
—GROUCHO MARX

---

HUMOR—Looking for and appreciating the humor all around us and even being able to laugh at one's self.

---

LET'S FACE IT—LIFE IS TOUGH SOMETIMES. WE FACE CHALLENGES every day. How do we get through each challenge unscathed? How do we move through life's labyrinth and keep our sanity? Honestly, humor is truly the best medicine!

I'm not suggesting walking through life with rose-colored glasses; I'm suggesting a light-hearted, humorous outlook on life. Even the most stressful situations have a funny side to them. A laugh or a smile can diffuse just about any difficult situation.

Humor can serve as a leveling force for the extremes we sometimes encounter, especially some extreme down times. In his book *Delivering Happiness: A Path to Profits, Passion, and Purpose,* Tony Hsieh says, "Things are never as bad or as good as they seem."[1]

When I was about eight years of age, my family was living in the Washington, DC area. One summer I had a special experience that formed one element of my personality—appreciating a sense of humor and figuring out how to use humor to connect with people.

Summers back then were to enjoy life as kids. One weekday, Dad asked if I'd like to go to work with him. He was the personnel director for United Airlines and worked at Washington National Airport. The plan was for me to go with him to his office for a couple hours, then we'd go into the city and have lunch and walk around a bit. This seemed like a grand adventure to me, and I really looked forward to a great day with my dad.

As we were walking to the car to go home, a large bird flew over me, crapped, and hit me right on the head. The crap oozed down the side of my head, around my ear, and then seeped down my neck onto my shoulder and disappeared inside my shirt. Yuck! Dad watched the whole nasty bird bombing.

He looked at me calmly and said, *"You know, for some people, they sing."*

He started laughing and handed me a cloth handkerchief (he always carried one, as I still do today too).

"You know, for some people, they sing."

As I wiped off the crap, he was still laughing. His laughter was contagious, and the "horror" of being crapped on by a bird turned to a very funny time together. We stood on the sidewalk laughing at what had happened and his response. I treasure that day with him and the beginning of being able to see the humor in many little bits of life.

In that example, while my initial reaction was shock, seeing the humor in the situation allowed me to keep the whole thing in perspective and laugh at it. As I grew up, humor has always been a part of my personality and the personalities of those I chose to be around.

Much later in life, I found myself working in (for me) a very difficult situation. These things often happen in organizations. The company was removing my boss from his position. I had a great working relationship with this man and we were doing great things together. We genuinely enjoyed working together. A new boss arrived on the scene. He was a nice man, but far less competent than my former boss, and I had a very hard time finding much respect for him. From the beginning, I struggled. After one of my most difficult meetings with him, I went back to my office and made a small sign that I kept on my desk for the next several years. I wrote, "KEEP THINGS IN PERSPECTIVE."

That simple sign and what it meant helped get me through many more difficult situations. By keeping things in the proper perspective, I was better able to see the humor in a lot of different circumstances. Laughing at a situation, or even at myself in that situation, has helped keep me grounded.

I admit that from an early age I seemed to derive joy from saying or doing something that would make others laugh.

THE 9 DIMENSIONS OF CONSCIOUS SUCCESS

Often, I would make myself the butt of the joke. This fifth differentiator is to keep things in perspective and not take yourself too seriously—make humor part of your demeanor. There is conflicting research about the old adage that it takes more muscles to frown than to smile. Regardless, there seems to be a lot of *face value* on the many notions of this idea.

## Smile Study

Whether it is physically less exhausting to smile than to scowl, it is certainly beneficial, and thus there is something to this ancient exhortation to put aside negative emotions long enough to "turn a frown upside down."

In a 2002 study performed in Sweden, researchers confirmed what our grandmothers already knew—people respond in kind to the facial expressions they encounter. In the study, test subjects were shown photos of faces—some smiling and some frowning—and were required to respond with their own smiles, frowns, and non-expressions as directed by those conducting the experiment.

Researchers noted that while folks had an easy time frowning at pictures that appeared to be frowning at them and smiling in reply to the photographed smiles, they had difficulty responding in an opposite manner to the expressions displayed in the images. The subjects instinctively wanted to reflect what they had been exposed to, answering smile for smile and frown for frown.

Facial expressions are contagious.

We are wired to instinctively respond like for like; facial expressions are contagious. When taken, the homily's implied advice to put on a happy face does work to benefit society in that smiling people cause those around them to smile.

Smiling is not just good for the community where the sad sack or grouch lives, it also benefits the person doing the grinning. Facial expressions do not merely signal what someone feels but actually contribute to that feeling. If we smile even when we don't feel like it, our mood will elevate despite ourselves. Likewise, faking a frown brings on a sense of not much liking the world that day.

Indeed, this cart-before-the-horse effect has been studied and measured by numerous researchers. It has been demonstrated that people who produced facial expressions of fear, anger, sadness, or disgust manifested the same bodily reactions that experiencing bouts of the actual emotions would have provoked (increased heart rate, elevated skin temperature, and sweating). Likewise, in studies of test subjects who were required to smile, compared to those who weren't, those instructed to force smiles onto their faces reported feeling happier than their non-grinning counterparts did. In both cases, although test subjects knew they were acting, their bodies didn't, and so their bodies responded accordingly. At least in this chapter of the saga of the mind against the body, the body won.

Smiling makes us feel happier. It isn't a cure-all for every situation (that is, don't look to it to remedy overwhelming grief), but in terms of getting us past a small dose of the blues, it can help to lift the sense of sadness.

# Physiological Changes

Ask yourself, *Would I rather be around people who smile and laugh on a regular basis?* The answer for most people is yes. Laughter actually makes us feel better—and on a physiological level, makes us healthier.

Endorphins are feel-good hormones in our body. They help:

- Promote a euphoric feeling

- Decrease depression

- Elevate our mood

- Enhance memory

- Produce a sense of satisfaction

- Reduce the stress hormone cortisol

- Expand our lungs and stretch the muscles in our body

- Release pent-up negative emotions

Smiling often can attract people to you. In social settings, it is a "grooming at a distance," which gives us a feeling of belonging and being taken care of.

# Inappropriate Humor

Not all humor is created equally. Different people have different standards of what they think is funny and, more importantly, what is appropriate. For example, humor at the expense of another's feelings, age, race, etc. backfires horribly. Humor should be victimless, harmless.

To determine what is acceptable in a particular group, listen to the conversations and go from there. It is much safer to observe than to jump in with a joke or story that immediately alienates you. This is especially true when you have joined a new team or are in a new social group.

**Right Time**: Is it the right time to tell a joke or be humorous? There are certain situations that demand seriousness. Telling jokes during a funeral in most, but not all, situations could be seen as disrespectful.

**Right Place**: Is it the right place to be humorous? Telling a joke in front of a judge during a traffic ticket hearing could receive a harsh response. That is not the place or time. Also, a joke you might have with a colleague may not be as well received in a client's office.

**Right Context**: Some situations just don't need humor, such as a serious management meeting. Humor can transform a room, and sometimes this is not a good thing. It can slow things down, and others judge your humor as a sign that you not taking a situation seriously.

Not everyone is funny, but that doesn't mean you don't appreciate humor. You can laugh and enjoy a humorous joke or story, even if you are not the source. You will be seen as easygoing and approachable. Having this personality trait is a definite, positive differentiator. Others will like being with you.

In addition, humor can be used as a deflector. A witty turn of phrase or gentle elbow to the rib with a smile can defuse a tense confrontation. If you have established a professionally friendly style, this tactic will be welcomed by colleagues.

## Humor as a Differentiator

To be good at humor shows intelligence, creativity, and creates a connection. I often employ humor in consulting situations and even in public speaking because it creates a connection with people and can make what I'm saying a lot more palatable. People like to laugh, and they like to be around people who make them laugh. There is an adage that people learn best when they are a bit entertained.

## Foundation Framework for Conscious Success

### *Purpose*

If you are a stand-up comedian, being funny is what you do. You are trying to be funny, and it is what others expect. Your purpose is to make people laugh.

In your job, is it necessary to be funny all the time? Sure it can lighten the mood of your coworkers, but is it your purpose? No.

Be sure the style and content of your humor is consistent with your purpose and brand. For example, if you are a surgeon, you wouldn't want to be cracking jokes in the middle of a serious surgery. You can have a sense of humor, but it must be consistent with your image and what it is you want to accomplish.

I'm not suggesting you need to be serious all the time to be respected. In fact, levity can garner more respect when leveraged correctly.

### Self-Awareness

Remember that humor is a great tool when used appropriately. You need self-awareness regarding how and when you use that tool. Are you being authentic? Are you hiding behind it? Is the humor you are using true to your intent and purpose?

Test yourself. Be sure you are good at humor. You don't need to be a clown in order to differentiate yourself. It is a tool that should be used strategically. Stick with what you are good at and you will shine. If you try to be humorous and you're not being authentic, others will notice and you will be viewed as "trying too hard." Be natural and organic with your funny side. Tell some jokes and stories to your family and friends—note their reactions. Usually those closest to us are the toughest audiences; if you can make them laugh, you're on the right track.

### Social Awareness

Look for social cues to how humor works, or doesn't work, at your place of business. Is there a light-hearted atmosphere in the office or work area? When you insert humor into a discussion, does it change the tone of the conversation?

When traveling recently, I stayed at a Marriott property. I love to observe people and, in some cases, give them feedback. The hospitality industry is a tough one. These people work long hours, make an hourly wage, and are at the forefront of complaints.

The manager was friendly with a smile, and so I immediately responded with a smile. She made a couple of jokes as I went through the process of checking in. It was very busy and some people were complaining about towels, but her smile and demeanor never faltered.

I had dinner that evening and the hostess took my order, as they were short staffed. She was openly friendly, even using some mild self-deprecating humor as she stepped out of her usual role. I felt attended to, and her attitude lightened my mood after a long day.

The second night I was there, I noticed that the manager had pizza delivered for the restaurant staff and they had a little pizza party in the back. They were laughing and having a great time. I commented on how well they got along and how happy they seemed.

The manager said, "I'm so glad you noticed. We're like a family here—we're all in this together. I ordered pizza because we needed some fun. We are way understaffed, but that doesn't mean we must suffer through it. We can support and laugh and have a good time."

I would love to work in that type of environment; it was perfect for the travel-weary customers who walked through their lobby every day.

## Now What?

Make a conscious effort to keep things in perspective. Try not to take yourself too seriously and practice smiling more often.

> "A day without sunshine is, like, you know, night."
>
> —STEVE MARTIN

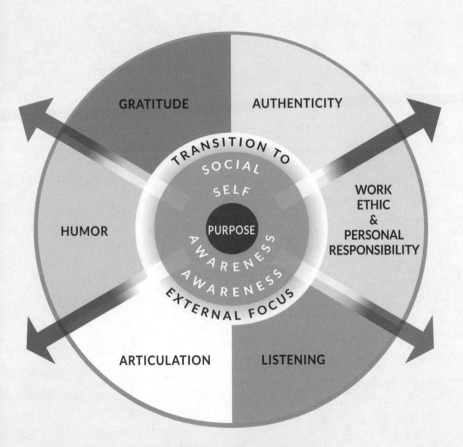

GRATITUDE

AUTHENTICITY

HUMOR

WORK
ETHIC
&
PERSONAL
RESPONSIBILITY

ARTICULATION

LISTENING

TRANSITION TO
SOCIAL
SELF
PURPOSE
AWARENESS
AWARENESS
EXTERNAL FOCUS

# DIFFERENTIATOR 6—
# GRATITUDE

# CHAPTER 10

# GRATITUDE

*"If I ain't happy here, I ain't happy nowhere."*
—Michael Hearne, "New Mexico Rain"

---

GRATITUDE—Making the choice to be thankful for what you have and consciously demonstrating gratitude when others do something for you.

---

THANK YOU FOR BUYING THIS BOOK AND READING THIS FAR, giving me a chance to share my thoughts about success. Your commitment is appreciated.

Over the years I've learned to be thankful for all that I have versus focusing on what I don't have. I'm a lot smarter about understanding *wants* versus *needs*.

> "You can't always get what you want, but if you try sometimes, you just might find, you get what you need."
>
> —Mick Jagger

Many people live blessed lives. That is not a religious reference but a reality that, for most of us, life is pretty good and generally we have more than we need. But we don't always pay attention to how blessed we truly are.

Years ago I read about a particular Native American tribe whose philosophy was not to pray for things they wanted but rather to give thanks for what they already had. That made a lot of sense to me, and I ascribe to it through frequent daily affirmations.

My good friend, Hyler Bracey, tries to live by the motto, *"Want what you have."* It's a great reminder for everyone.

When I talk about gratitude, I focus on two areas. First is the basic orientation or attitude we can wake up with each morning. The second is how we demonstrate gratitude in an authentic way in our interactions.

There are several influences that cause me to include gratitude as an important differentiator. My mother and father and German grandmother (who lived with us and was one of the nicest people I've ever known) emphasized that saying thank you was expected. It was more than just being polite; it was part of everyday life growing up. So saying thank you, showing gratitude and appreciation, was an early lesson learned. More on that later.

1.  Being thankful every day for what you have vs. what you don't have or wish you had.

2.  Consciously saying thank you for even the smallest things that are done for you or to support you.

# Daily Gratitude

Gratitude is about attitude. It is the mindset you wake up with every morning and it guides your outlook on the world. I make a conscious effort to be positive and thankful for what I have.

Gratitude is a conscious choice. It doesn't just happen. You have to think and act on it. You have to take stock of your life and appreciate all the wonderful things in it. The alternative is to focus on what is *not* going right, which produces a gloomy outlook and attitude.

> Gratitude is about attitude.

Being grateful gets you a lot further in life than the alternative. Having a positive outlook actually makes you more attractive to others. It is hard for people not to notice a smile on your face.

Studies by psychologist Robert Emmons and others have shown that those who demonstrate gratitude are more energetic, emotionally intelligent, forgiving, and less likely to be depressed, anxious, or lonely. Gratitude not only makes us feel happier, it is a significant cause of positive outcomes.

A gratitude orientation produces measurable results in your life and enhances your performance. Gratitude links to a positive attitude that we covered in Chapter 1. You are more pleasant to be around, which sets you apart from the pessimists. Seeing the good in life allows you to avoid being judgmental and promotes *unconditional positive regard* (UPR), which acts as a relationship accelerator.

# Gratitude for Others

Psychologist Abraham H. Maslow was famous for creating the hierarchy of needs. Each tier represents a set of needs that most humans share. The most basic needs are on the bottom and go to the top of self-actualization. Unless the needs of a particular tier are satisfied, it is not possible to move up to the next level.

The need to belong is a basic need we all share. We want to be part of a group and to be appreciated by others in that group. Showing someone gratitude is a powerful way to meet that need.

> "Help people reach their full potential—catch them doing something right."
> —KENNETH H. BLANCHARD,
> *The One Minute Manager*

In order to motivate and lead others, we need two things in our tool belt—a carrot (gratitude) and a stick (discipline). The stick is easy to employ and often leads to micromanaging and resentment by employees. The stick has to be used sometimes, but should be used carefully and very sparingly.

On the other hand, the carrot is so much more effective in motivating others. It is as simple as saying, "Thank you for doing a good job." It's well-documented that when we use positive reinforcement for a specific desired behavior, it dramatically improves the probability the person will repeat the behavior. Showing gratitude is a positive reinforcement.

Research indicates it take a ratio of 4 positive reinforcement experiences to 1 negative reinforcement experience for the recipient to believe they get an equal amount of positive and negative reinforcement.

Everyone likes to feel appreciated. It is imprinted in our DNA. It is a need, not just something nice. Without it, we feel isolated, depressed, and like an outsider.

Showing appreciation for others also makes us feel better ourselves. You probably know of the character Scrooge in the story *A Christmas Carol*. In the beginning, Scrooge was not grateful for anything. He didn't appreciate his employee and he didn't appreciate his family. In both cases, he was critical and even mean, and in return he felt even worse about himself. He was lonely and crotchety, and even money did not bring him any joy because he thought he never had enough of it.

> Bah humbug!

As the story goes, he was visited first by his dead partner and then by three spirits that showed him his life from a different perspective. He was shown things that he should have appreciated and where his life would end if he continued being ungrateful.

The next morning when he awoke, he was transformed. He had learned about gratitude and had a sudden appreciation for life. He gave his employee a raise and the day off, then bought food and presents for his nephew and family and joined them in a Christmas dinner, an invitation he had refused for many years. He felt the joy of giving and he transformed people's lives with his gratitude.

I recently read an article about appreciation called "My Eight Dollar Flight Upgrade Trick." written by Peter Shankman, founder of HARO. I thought, like you might be thinking right now, that he was referring to some loophole to get a better seat on a plane or being bumped up to first class. But he was actually referring to an oversized bag of M&Ms candy.

In the article, Shankman says he receives an upgrade in service, no matter where he is sitting, by simply bringing a bag of M&Ms on the plane and handing it to the head flight attendant. The only caveat is that the candy must be shared with the other flight attendants.

He does this to show his appreciation for all the hard work and many hours the flight crew spend to make a safe and enjoyable flight. He says it works every time, not only for him, but for all the passengers. His act of appreciation lightens the load a bit for the crew and changes their mood, and that translates to smiles and better service.

What do you do to show appreciation and gratitude for others around you?

When you acknowledge others for their hard work and you thank them for it, they also appreciate the fruits of their labor. They work hard and they are rewarded for it. They don't just expect things—they earn them. Gratitude is infectious, and, like a virus, when it touches people it changes them at an almost molecular level. When people are inspired and acknowledged, people are transformed.

When children say please and thank you, people think, *What well-mannered children. They must have been brought up by good parents.* The opposite is also true.

Adults know how to say please and thank you. What does it cost us? A moment of time. Yet that time is well spent. I have heard people tell leaders if they praise their team too much, they will be seen as soft and ineffective. I have to politely disagree. No harm has ever come from telling someone thank you.

# Framework for Conscious Success

## *Purpose*

Gratitude drives your purpose. Part of my personal purpose is to be appreciative. I am aware of people doing a good job and I acknowledge them for it. This ties directly to *social awareness.*

> When gratitude is at odds with your purpose, you risk your intent being at odds with your impact.

An example is a client with whom I worked recently. He is highly intelligent, and he lets everyone know that he is. He is tyrannical and prone to outbursts of anger, and he has a tendency to put people down by wielding his power as someone in charge.

I doubt he wants people to see him as unappreciative, but that is how he is perceived. Even if he showed some appreciation for others, the gesture is overshadowed by his general abrasive and condescending demeanor.

If his purpose is to get fired because no one wants to work with him, then I guess he is right on track. It would take a lot of pleases and thank yous for him to make a different impact, but it can be done.

How do you think gratitude fits into your purpose? How are you delivering that gratitude every day?

## *Self-Awareness*

In my example of the intelligent dictator, what level of self-awareness does that person have? Does he enjoy making people dislike him? How do you think people see you—as appreciative of them or too self-absorbed to see the good in them?

As I have already mentioned, gratitude is a conscious and willful action. You have to be aware of what you have in life for which you should be grateful. Once you have identified all your blessings, then remember and renew your gratitude for each one daily. Thankfulness is the sun in the morning fog—gratitude will burn away any doubts you have about your purpose in life.

## *Social Awareness*

You must be aware of whether your intent matches your impact. If you want to differentiate yourself from the crowd, you must build solid relationships with others. People are attracted to those who show them gratitude and appreciation and respect for their skills, their ideas, and even their time. Showing someone gratitude is the same as showing them respect; this is highly regarded in business and in any relationship.

Be aware of how you interact with others and how that can affect all your relationships. A colleague told me about the time she went to lunch with a client who was rude to the server.

"Can't you see we're busy? We will call you when we are ready for you," was the client's opening statement. My colleague was shocked. About ten minutes later the server came back, and again the client was rude.

"I told you I would call you when we're ready. I'm having a business meeting and you are interrupting. Is there something wrong with your ability to understand what I'm telling you?"

My colleague had had enough. She said to the server, "Listen, I know you're working hard and you rely on tips to make a living. So please give me five minutes. At the end of those five minutes, either we will be ready to order, or you will have only me to serve."

She then turned to the client and said, "I really would love to do business with you, but what you demonstrated to me is a lack of gratitude, respect, and grace. I don't know if I can work with someone like that. I worked as a wait person for many years, and it was hard. We got paid a couple dollars an hour and we relied on providing a great service in order to receive a tip. That waiter did nothing but ask us for our drink order. So either you apologize for your behavior or I'm leaving."

I know this sounds like a bold move, but the outcome may surprise you. The client said she was so used to treating wait staff like that, she thought it was expected. She didn't realize they were paid so little, and she admitted she was acting like she was in control in order to impress my colleague. Her impact was way off base from her intent.

The happy end of the story is that the client apologized many times to the server, left an enormous tip, and they ended up doing business together.

## Why Don't People Say Thank You?

We know that saying please and thank you is the right thing. We know we like it when someone else shows us gratitude. We know we like to see someone smile when we show them gratitude.

Why don't more people practice gratitude? Here are five top reasons from my experience:

1. It's not a priority. We forget about the impact it has. If we make gratitude a habit, then it becomes a daily priority.

2. We assume people know. You might know someone is happy with your work and dedication, but isn't it nice to hear it?

3. Impatience and being in a hurry.

4. Low social awareness—unaware of just how important it is to most others.

5 Rudeness is probably rare but it does occur and sometimes without much social awareness.

## Now What?

1. In his book *The Happiness Advantage*, Shawn Achor suggests a simple technique to promote a more positive outlook. He suggests either by yourself or with someone else to consciously identify three things you are grateful for each day. Get in the habit of doing this each day for a week and you will improve the probability of it becoming a habit. Use the three gratitudes per day to promote a more positive outlook.

2. Track the times you say thank you; be aware of when you do and when you don't—and when you should.

3. Ask those closest to you how they see you in terms of gratitude and how appreciative you are of others.

"Do not spoil what you have by desiring what you have not; remember that what you now have was once among the things you only hoped for."

—EPICURUS

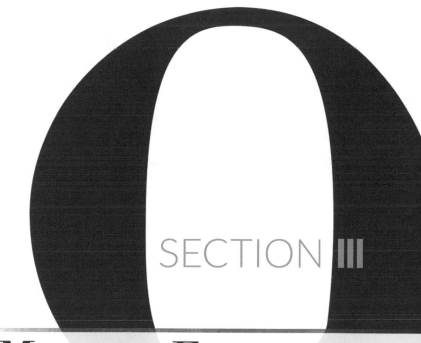

# SECTION ▌▌▌

# MOVING FORWARD
# SUCCESSFULLY

# CHAPTER 11

# CONSCIOUS ACTION PLAN

WHEN FINALIZING THE CONCEPT FOR THIS BOOK, I KNEW I wanted it to be a very practical, data-driven guide, ensuring readers would want to take action to make improvements. As my mentor John Jones would say, *"Awareness precedes meaningful choice."*

Think back to my story about learning to waterski. What was missing was a *structure* to follow and *consciousness* of my effort.

It is my sincerest hope that in reading this book you have begun to develop a structure to follow, and all it takes is a conscious effort to make it happen. One significant takeaway should be from the concept *100 percent responsibility*. You and you alone are 100 percent responsible for producing the desired result.

A number of years ago, I came across a poem by Dale Wimbrow that provides a strong message of personal responsibility. I like it a lot and find it to be a clever reinforcement that as we march through life we are most accountable to ourselves. I share this poem with you and hope it inspires you as it has me.

## The Guy in the Glass

by Dale Wimbrow, © 1934

*When you get what you want in*
*your struggle for pelf,*
*And the world makes you King for a day,*
*Then go to the mirror and look at yourself,*
*And see what that guy has to say.*
*For it isn't your Father, or Mother, or Wife,*
*Who judgement upon you must pass.*
*The feller whose verdict counts most in your life*
*Is the guy staring back from the glass.*
*He's the feller to please, never mind all the rest,*
*For he's with you clear up to the end,*
*And you've passed your most dangerous, difficult test*
*If the guy in the glass is your friend.*
*You may be like Jack Horner and "chisel" a plum,*
*And think you're a wonderful guy,*
*But the man in the glass says you're only a bum*
*If you can't look him straight in the eye.*
*You can fool the whole world down*
*the pathway of years,*
*And get pats on the back as you pass,*
*But your final reward will be heartaches and tears*
*If you've cheated the guy in the glass.*

Early in the book you learned of the three foundational elements that support you (purpose, self-awareness, social awareness), and then you learned of the six essential differentiators that enable you to stand out among your peers (authenticity, work ethic and responsibility, listening, communicating, humor, gratitude).

Within each of the differentiators, you learned not only how each manifests, but also how each can be improved to bolster your platform and visibility in the workplace. The next step is to use your new-found knowledge to improve your life.

You may be excited about making some changes. You may talk about what you've learned, ready to put what you learned to work for you. Great! You have to focus on your goal—keeping track of the progress and dedicating each day to moving forward.

When I was hyped about writing this book, I started out full of enthusiasm. And then, life happened and priorities shifted. Other important issues took my attention, and poof—two months faded away. How did I accomplish my goal? I *consciously shifted my focus* back to writing.

> It happens on purpose—for a purpose.

It takes commitment, focus, and a force of will to plug a new framework into your life. It doesn't happen by accident; it happens on purpose. From *commitment* (to a goal), *focus* (on achieving that goal), and *force of will* (creating action on achieving that goal) the foundation framework for conscious success is formulated.

This last chapter is dedicated to the conscious success framework. I could try to dazzle you with some unverified quote about how the most successful people in the world achieved their success by writing down their goals and plans. And the fact is, if you write it down, you are more likely to get it done.

Why is that a fact? When you write something on a piece of paper, it creates permanence. Unless you spill coffee on it or accidentally set it on fire, the words remain intact—they do not run around the page of their own volition to create new words.

Our brains do not operate in that level of permanence, as our thoughts, intentions, and attention are constantly shifting. Written plans are reminders, stable nonmoving reminders of what we have committed to achieve.

- We commit to a goal by writing it down (commitment).

- The words we write are permanent reminders (focus).

- When we read our plan to reach our goals, we focus on our commitment and are reminded what we need to do (force of will).

## Commitment

A digital copy of the template for a Conscious Action Plan can be downloaded from www.conscioussuccess.com. Use the following steps or guidelines to create your plan.

1. Choose one of the differentiators you wish to work on from the previous chapters. Choose only one at a time to focus on. State what the

differentiator is and turn it into a goal statement. The statement should always be in the positive, not the negative. For instance, you would write, "I will reach my optimum weight of 130 pounds in six months" rather than "I want to drop thirty pounds." Also notice that there is a timeline for achievement, which is essential and makes the goal measurable. Goals that are not measurable: "I intend to use more humor in the workplace." That statement is vague. Instead write, "My performance evaluation six months from now will have at least two or three comments characterizing me as fun or easygoing, as well as professionally friendly." Finally, your goals need to be realistic and achievable. While it is important to challenge ourselves, no one is motivated by consistent failure to achieve goals. I love opportunities to grow, but I also love opportunities to celebrate success.

2. Choose one to three actions you intend to exhibit every day in order to reach your goal. Again, these must be measurable. Looking at the humor example, it is not good enough to say, "I'm going to be funnier today." Instead, an action statement would be, "I'm going to smile whenever I begin a conversation." Smiles have a way of being contagious. It is important that you do not choose more than three actions, as your ability to focus and manifest each will become diffused.

3.  Create a review process. This process must work for the goals and actions you create, so there is no one-system-fits-all approach. In some cases, you need to measure your success and periodically review your results. In other cases, you may need an external process such as a review or survey performed by your clients or colleagues. The important components of a review:

    a.  You must review on a regular and scheduled basis.

    b.  The data must be verifiable.

    c.  You must take the data and make new, actionable changes to your plan.

## Focus

What good is a framework or plan if it is buried in a folder or desk drawer? Out of sight, out of mind. Once you have created your plan, you must see it as a living, breathing document that you refer to often. You can condense parts from the plan, such as the action steps, and write them on notecards or sticky notes. Place them on your computer, bathroom mirror, or even your dashboard to serve as prompts for focusing on them. If you are like me, you have a million things running through your mind during the day, each vying for your attention. Having written reminders is a great way to store information outside all of the brain chatter.

Another suggestion is to write your goals and deadlines on your calendar:

■   March 7: Review my goals on authenticity.

■ March 10, 6:45 A.M.: Write three things I'm grateful for today.

The point is that you need your goals and action steps in front of you to be sure they remain a focus throughout the chaos of a typical day.

## Force of Will

Being consciously aware and willful about our actions is really at the heart of this book. Successful differentiation does not happen by a runaway truck striking us at an intersection. It is about attentive observation (the three foundational elements), understanding how to stand out (the differentiators), and then taking the actions necessary to get the job done (improving your life).

There are plenty of books that provide excellent advice. There are plenty of professional speakers who espouse life-changing ideas and concepts. There are brilliant coaches and consultants who have the knowledge and experience to change people's lives—but not one of these people or books alone can change anything. They have no mystical power. They are not a pharmaceutical cocktail that can be injected.

There is only one person who has the knowledge, the experience, and the power to change your life—the one staring at you in the mirror. My hope is that this book has provided you tools and a path toward your personal and professional goals. You have the power to make positive changes in your life—go for it!

# What Next?

Step out into a new world of unlimited possibilities and grab each opportunity that comes your way. No one can keep you from becoming the person you set your mind on becoming. Take one more review of the Conscious Success Model.

As you begin living your life according to these ideals and objectives, there will be gradual but very noticeable changes around you. The problems you have in your life will turn to challenges and then turn to opportunities. The worries you carry will start seeming a bit less important and heavy until soon you will be able to change your perspective on them the instant they come into your mind. You will begin to see more positive in people and in turn begin to attract more positive and like-minded people into your life.

The growth and learning process will continue throughout the entirety of your life, and you'll find no greater joy than this experience.

Remember the words of Nelson Mandela, who said, "It's always impossible until it's done."

# INTERVIEW SURVEY RESULTS

**Question 1**: Think of one or two very successful (in business and life) individuals you've witnessed/admired in your career. What two or three personality traits in those successful individuals do you believe most contributed to their success.

☐ Good outlook with well-defined values

☐ Sensitive to other people and work well with others

☐ Stick to one's beliefs

☐ Strong commitment to what was done and were driven without being excessive

☐ Positive attitude

☐ Were able to hear bad news as well as good news

☐ Ability to relate to people

☐ Built-in tenacity to succeed

☐ Strong work ethic

☐ Had integrity, not just honesty

☐ Personal accountability

☐ Humility

☐ Care about others

☐ Balance of work and life

☐ Willingness to make time for others

☐ Never doubted that they would do what they set out to do, and assumed they would learn

☐ Dedicated to the company

☐ Took time to be self-aware and not robotic

☐ Great listeners

☐ Having a great sense of humor

☐ Consensus-driven

☐ Didn't live in their past and were optimistic about their future

☐ Great communication skills

☐ Able to motivate and inspire

☐ Enormous capacity for compassion and empathy

☐ Down to earth

**Question 2**: What two or three qualities or personality traits have most contributed to your own success in business and in life?

☐ Relating well with others

☐ Easy to talk to

☐ Hard-working

☐ Persistent

☐ Sense of humor

☐ Strong work ethic

☐ Find the best in others; look for the pearl in everyone

☐ Have ego in check

☐ Wandered around to catch people doing things right

☐ Adaptability

☐ Willingness to do what was necessary

☐ Willing to color outside the lines

☐ Ability to listen

☐ Situational awareness

☐ Observational skills

☐ Passion for helping people move from where they are toward success

☐ Let others get the credit

☐ Always took advantage of opportunities as they presented themselves

☐ Long-term goal setting

☐ Kindness

☐ Being accountable

☐ Admit mistakes

☐ Self-awareness

☐ Honesty and authenticity

☐ Having a clear understanding of who I am, because that does not change over time

☐ Having a clear understanding of my beliefs and values

☐ Good communication skills

☐ Embraced challenges

**Question 3**: What behaviors or personality traits do you believe most hinders others in being successful in life and in business?

☐ Being narrow-minded

☐ Poor people-skills

☐ Tunnel vision

☐ Inflexibility

☐ Focusing on yourself rather than others

☐ Lack of drive and self-confidence

☐ Entitlement attitude

☐ Lack of interpersonal skills

☐ Inability to ask for help

☐ Lack of patience

☐ Lack of humility

☐ Lack of motivation

☐ Blaming others

☐ Lack of accountability

☐ Self-centeredness

☐ Lack of awareness of others

☐ Not being able to think strategically

☐ Being reactive rather than proactive

☐ Unable to take risks

☐ Inability to delay gratification

☐ Being rigid

☐ Lack of ethics

☐ Lack of honesty

☐ Lack of faith in self

☐ Lack of focus

**Question 4**: When considering one of your most challenging times or a time when you made a mistake and had to deal with it in the best way, what action or characteristic or thought helped you get through the adversity?

☐ Communicating well with others

☐ Self-reflection

- [ ] Support of others

- [ ] Admit a mistake and apologize

- [ ] Have a sense of humor

- [ ] Keep things in perspective

- [ ] Ask for help

- [ ] Be personally accountable

- [ ] Have hope that things would get better

- [ ] Step back for perspective

- [ ] Take a breath

- [ ] Survivor mindset—in adversity we learn who we really are

- [ ] Remove as much emotion as possible

- [ ] Consider the long view versus the short view

- [ ] Persistence

- [ ] Learn from it and move on

- [ ] A sense I could be forgiven

- [ ] Make amends

- [ ] Have someone close who believes in you

**Question 5**: What are the one or two most import-ant pieces of advice you would give to the next generation to improve their impact on our world in the future?

☐  Stop and listen

☐  Do something that contributes to society

☐  Work hard and do your best

☐  Leadership must be a side-by-side relationship

☐  Learn who you are and be relational as you do everything

☐  Learn to avoid the superficial

☐  Identify and adhere to your core values

☐  Don't become distracted

☐  Learn from your mistakes or you are doomed to repeat them

☐  When you enter the real world, there will be adversity

☐  Be clear on your focus

☐  You are responsible for the outcomes in your life

☐  Blame is not terribly helpful

☐  Learn how to let it go

- ☐ Seek always to do the right thing, not necessarily what is the most expedient

- ☐ Be a self-advocate

- ☐ Don't lose your sense of humor

- ☐ Have an attitude of gratitude

- ☐ You don't get a trophy for just participating in life

- ☐ Be competitive, and when you lose, learn from it and fight smarter next time

- ☐ Be true to yourself

- ☐ Use mentors in your life

- ☐ Find a cause beyond yourself where you can make an impact

- ☐ Nothing is given you; you have to work at it

- ☐ Seek to know and understand more than you do

The following is a tally of the number of times each word or phrase was used in the interviewee responses.

## Question 1

- Purpose—33

- Social Awareness—27

- Belief Systems and Values—25

- Application and Implementation—19

- Communication and Listening—23

- Leadership and Mentorship—14

- Flexibility—13

- Humility—9

- Knowledge—12

- Self-Awareness—8

- Independence—2

## Question 2

- Purpose—46

- Belief Systems and Values—18

- Social Awareness—21

- Application and Implementation—19

- Communication and Listening—17

- Leadership and Mentorship—15

- Flexibility—15

- Humility—11

- Knowledge—11

- Self-Awareness—9

## *Question 3*

- Purpose—20

- Belief Systems and Values—25

- Social Awareness—23

- Application and Implementation—6

- Communication and Listening—10

- Leadership and Mentorship  8

- Flexibility—15

- Humility—18

- Knowledge—4

- Self-Awareness—1

## *Question 4*

- Purpose—25

- Belief Systems and Values—35

- Social Awareness—3

- Application and Implementation—10

- Communication and Listening—3

- Leadership and Mentorship—0

- Flexibility—3

- Humility—9

- Knowledge—4

- Self-Awareness—4

- Support System—14

## *Question 5*

- Purpose—20

- Belief Systems and Values—19

- Social Awareness—20

- Application and Implementation—13

- Communication and Listening—9

- Leadership and Mentorship—7

- Flexibility—8

- Humility—6

- Knowledge—12

- Self-Awareness—11

# MY PURPOSE
# STATEMENT

DEFINING YOUR PURPOSE IS NO SMALL THING. IT REQUIRES thought and living with it for a bit as we've discussed. This Personal Purpose Statement is really what you are about and how you wish to engage your life on the planet.

Here is a process or template for building your own Personal Purpose Statement.

## MY PERSONAL PURPOSE STATEMENT

1.  Make a list of your core values. Examples might be Honesty, Integrity, Compassion, Empathy, Fun, Laughter, Hard Work, Health. These are just examples—think hard and truly make them your own.

2.  Now Make a list of the things you believe you are good at. It might be a good idea to seek some external feedback on how others see what you are good at. Use trusted people and just ask.

3.  Now make a list of the things you really like doing. Focus mostly on work activities. Focus mostly on the things from which you might make a living. By the way, things you do for fun might be fair game if you could make a living from that. Rank the top three from most to least enjoyment.

4.  For the top three things you selected—list what specifically you like about that activity or Item.

5. Now the hard part—from Items 1-4 look for themes and patterns which emerge for "What you are all about." List those themes/patterns.

6.  Based on the themes and patterns, write a draft *Personal Purpose Statement*

7.  Live with your draft statement for one week. Check it each morning and notice whatever you notice—make changes as you see fit. Let this "life editing" process just happen for the week.

8.  Finalize your Purpose Statement and begin to internalize/memorize it.

9.  In the weeks to come—"socialize" your statement with people close to you to lock it down.

## *My Life Purpose is...*

_____

_____

_____

_____

_____

_____

_____

_____

_____

_____

_____

_____

# A MESSAGE TO GARCIA

By Elbert Hubbard

*First published in 1899, this essay has been translated into many languages and carries a powerful message that has been read by generations of scholars, students, and people of all races, creeds, careers, and status. Widely considered as one of the greatest classics of all time.*

IN ALL THIS CUBAN BUSINESS THERE IS ONE MAN STANDS OUT on the horizon of my memory like Mars at perihelion.

When war broke out between Spain and the United States, it was very necessary to communicate quickly with the leader of the insurgents. Garcia was somewhere in the mountain vastness of Cuba—no one knew where. No mail nor telegraph message could reach him. The President must secure his cooperation, and quickly.

What to do!

Someone said to the President, "There's a fellow by the name of Rowan will find Garcia for you, if anybody can."

Rowan was sent for and given a letter to be delivered to Garcia. How "the fellow by the name of Rowan" took the letter, sealed it up in an oil-skin pouch, strapped it over his heart, in four days landed by night off the coast of Cuba from an open boat, disappeared into the jungle, and in three weeks came out on the other side of the island, having traversed a hostile country on foot, and delivered his letter to Garcia, are things I have no special desire now to tell in detail.

The point I wish to make is this: McKinley gave Rowan a letter to be delivered to Garcia; Rowan took the letter and did not ask, "Where is he at?" By the Eternal! There is a man whose form should be cast in deathless bronze and the statue placed in every college of the land. It is not book-learning young men need, nor instruction about this and that, but a stiffening of the vertebrae which will cause them to be loyal to a trust, to act promptly, concentrate their energies: do the thing—"Carry a message to Garcia!"

General Garcia is dead now, but there are other Garcias.

No man, who has endeavored to carry out an enterprise where many hands were needed, but has been well-nigh appalled at times by the imbecility of the average man—the inability or unwillingness to concentrate on a thing and do it. Slip-shod assistance, foolish inattention, dowdy indifference, and half-hearted work seem the rule; and no man succeeds, unless by hook or crook, or threat, he forces or bribes other men to assist him; or mayhap, God in His goodness performs a miracle, and sends him an Angel of Light for an assistant.

You, reader, put this matter to a test:

You are sitting now in your office—six clerks are within call. Summon anyone and make this request: "Please look in the encyclopedia and make a brief memorandum for me concerning the life of Correggio."

Will the clerk quietly say, "Yes, sir," and go do the task?

On your life, he will not. He will look at you out of a fish eye and ask one or more of the following questions:

Who was he?

Which encyclopedia?

Where is the encyclopedia?

Was I hired for that?

Don't you mean Bismarck?

What's the matter with Charlie doing it?

Is he dead?

Is there any hurry?

Shan't I bring you the book and let you look it up yourself?

What do you want to know for?

And I will lay you ten to one that after you have answered the questions, and explained how to find the information, and why you want it, the clerk will go off and get one of the other clerks to help him try to find Garcia—and then come back and tell you there is no such man. Of course I may lose my bet, but according to the Law of Average, I will not.

THE 9 DIMENSIONS OF CONSCIOUS SUCCESS

Now if you are wise you will not bother to explain to your "assistant" that Correggio is indexed under the C's, not in the K's, but you will smile sweetly and say, "Never mind," and go look it up yourself.

And this incapacity for independent action, this moral stupidity, this infirmity of the will, this unwillingness to cheerfully catch hold and lift, are the things that put pure Socialism so far into the future. If men will not act for themselves, what will they do when the benefit of their effort is for all? A first-mate with knotted club seems necessary; and the dread of getting "the bounce" Saturday night, holds many a worker to his place.

Advertise for a stenographer, and nine out of ten who apply, can neither spell nor punctuate—and do not think it necessary to.

Can such a one write a letter to Garcia?

"You see that bookkeeper," said the foreman to me in a large factory.

"Yes, what about him?"

"Well he's a fine accountant, but if I'd send him up town on an errand, he might accomplish the errand all right, and on the other hand, might stop at four saloons on the way, and when he got to Main Street, would forget what he had been sent for."

Can such a man be entrusted to carry a message to Garcia?

We have recently been hearing much maudlin sympathy expressed for the "downtrodden denizen of the sweat-shop" and the "homeless wanderer searching for honest employment," and with it all often go many hard words for the men in power.

Nothing is said about the employer who grows old before his time in a vain attempt to get frowsy ne'er-do-wells to do intelligent work; and his long patient striving with "help" that does nothing but loaf when his back is turned. In every store and factory there is a constant weeding-out process going on. The employer is constantly sending away "help" that have shown their incapacity to further the interests of the business, and others are being taken on. No matter how good times are, this sorting continues; only if times are hard and work is scarce, the sorting is done finer—but out and forever out, the incompetent and unworthy go. It is the survival of the fittest. Self-interest prompts every employer to keep the best—those who can carry a message to Garcia.

I know one man of really brilliant parts who has not the ability to manage a business of his own, and yet who is absolutely worthless to anyone else, because he carries with him constantly the insane suspicion that his employer is oppressing, or intending to oppress him. He cannot give orders; and he will not receive them. Should a message be given him to take to Garcia, his answer would probably be, "Take it yourself."

Tonight this man walks the streets looking for work, the wind whistling through his threadbare coat. No one who knows him dare employ him, for he is a regular fire-brand of discontent. He is impervious to reason, and the only thing that can impress him is the toe of a thick-soled No. 9 boot.

Of course I know that one so morally deformed is no less to be pitied than a physical cripple; but in our pitying, let us drop a tear, too, for the men who are striving to carry on a great enterprise, whose working hours are not limited by the whistle, and whose hair is fast turning white through the struggle to hold in line dowdy indifference, slip-shod imbecility, and the heartless ingratitude, which, but for their enterprise, would be both hungry and homeless.

Have I put the matter too strongly? Possibly I have; but when all the world has gone a-slumming I wish to speak a word of sympathy for the man who succeeds—the man who, against great odds has directed the efforts of others, and having succeeded, finds there's nothing in it: nothing but bare board and clothes.

I have carried a dinner pail and worked for day's wages, and I have also been an employer of labor, and I know there is something to be said on both sides. There is no excellence, per se, in poverty; rags are no recommendation; and all employers are not rapacious and high-handed, any more than all poor men are virtuous.

My heart goes out to the man who does his work when the "boss" is away, as well as when he is at home. And the man who, when given a letter for Garcia, quietly take the missive, without asking any idiotic questions, and with no lurking intention of chucking it into the nearest sewer, or of doing aught else but deliver it, never gets "laid off," nor has to go on a strike for higher wages. Civilization is one long anxious search for just such individuals. Anything such a man asks shall be granted; his kind is so rare that no employer can afford to let him go. He is wanted in every city, town, and village—in every office, shop, store, and factory. The world cries out for such: he is needed, and needed badly—the man who can carry a message to Garcia.[1]

# CHAPTER 2 ANSWER PAGE
## (Questions from page 36)

**Question 1:** Think of one or two very successful (in business and life) individuals you've witnessed/admired in your career. What two or three personality traits in those successful individuals do you believe most contributed to their success?

_____

_____

_____

_____

_____

**Question 2:** What two or three qualities or personality traits have most contributed to your own success in business and in life?

_____

_____

_____

_____

_____

**Question 3:** What behaviors or personality traits do you believe most hinder others in being successful in life and in business?

_____

_____

_____

_____

_____

**Question 4:** When considering one of your most challenging times or a time when you made a mistake and had to deal with it in the best way, what action or characteristic or thought helped you get through the adversity?

_____

_____

_____

_____

_____

**Question 5:** What are the one or two most important pieces of advice you would give to the next generation to improve their impact on our world in the future?

_____

_____

_____

_____

_____

_____

# Chapter 1

1. Bureau of Labor Statistics; Databases, Tables & Calculators by Subject; "CPI Inflation Calculator," accessed May 25, 2017, http://www.bls.gov/data/inflation_calculator.htm.

2. NUMBEO, "Cost of Living in United States," accessed May 25, 2017, http://www.numbeo.com/cost-of-living/country _result.jsp?country=United+States.

3. Heidi Shierholz, "Unemployment rate reaches highest level in over 14 years (Jobs Picture, November 7, 2008)," Economic Policy Institute, November, 2008, http://www.epi.org/ publication/webfeatures_econindicators_jobspict_20081107/.

4. *Oxford English Dictionary*, s.v. "Success," accessed July 13, 2017, https://en.oxforddictionaries.com/definition/success.

# Chapter 2

1. Merriam-Webster.com, s.v. "Sine qua Non," accessed July 13, 2017, https://www.merriam-webster.com/dictionary/ sine%20qua%20non.

# Chapter 3

1. General Electric, "Thomas Edition & the History of Electricity," accessed May 26, 2017, https://www.ge.com/ about-us/history/thomas-edison.

2. Lewis Carroll, *Alice's Adventures in Wonderland* (New York: Bantam Books, 1981), 49-50.

3.    Travis Bradberry and Jean Greaves, *Emotional Intelligence 2.0* (San Diego, CA: TalentSmart, 2009).
4.    Ibid.

## Chapter 6

1.    2015 data from the Organization for Economic Cooperation and Development (OECD).
2.    Colin Powell, *It Worked for Me: In Life and Leadership* (New York, Harper Perennial, 2014).

## Chapter 7

1.    Stephen R. Covey, *The 7 Habits of Highly Effective People: Powerful Lessons in Personal Change* (New York: Simon & Schuster, 1999).

## Chapter 8

1.    David K. Israel, "7 Curious Facts About 7 Dr. Seuss Books," Mental Floss, September 09, 2010, http://mentalfloss.com/article/25720/7-curious-facts-about-7-dr-seuss-books.
2.    Edward B. Fry and Jacqueline E. Kress, *The Reading Teacher's Book of Lists* (Indianapolis, IN: Jossey-Bass, 2006).

## Chapter 9

1.    Tony Hsieh, *Delivering Happiness: A Path to Profits, Passion, and Purpose* (New York, Grand Central Publishing, 2013).

## Appendix C

1.    Elbert Hubbard, *A Message to Garcia* (1899). Reprinted in *Annals of America,* Vol. 12, "1895-1904, Populism, Imperialism, and Reform" (Encyclopedia Britannica, 1976), 309-311.

# DAVID NIELSON
# & ASSOCIATES

**DAVID NIELSON & ASSOCIATES** (DNA) is a management consulting firm specializing in the execution of business strategy implementation and large-scale change. We educate, coach, and consult with organizations on how to create and sustain a change-adaptive culture to improve implementation success.

David Nielson brings over three decades of corporate, Fortune 500, and private consulting experience in organizational change management, leadership development, and training. David has helped guide large-scale change initiatives and business strategy driven by ERP, mergers, restructuring, and the need for cultural change. He has been a featured and frequent speaker at PMI, project World, Chief Executive Network, Management Resources Association, TEC, Training Director's Forum, and the Alliance of Organizational Systems Designers. Formerly managing director of the boutique management/consulting firm IMA, David specialized in strategic change and accelerating implementation, which helped lead IMA to annual double-digit growth. He served as Director of Organization Development and Manager of Sales and Marketing Planning at Coors Brewing Company, with an emphasis on sales management, training, and organizational development. In this role he successfully led a large culture change initiative and developed an overarching development curriculum for all functions within the business.

A co-founder of the Denver OD Network Chapter, David is a community leader and has served on the boards of Red Rocks Community College, the National Pain Foundation, and is a former Chairman of the Board of Directors of the Colorado Boys' Ranch.